People Are Talking About QUEEN MOM . . .

"*Queen Mom* is the most encouraging book about parenting I have ever read. Brimming with practical examples and biblical truth, it illustrates how to be the mom God has called me to be—from my children's toddler years through their teenage years. If I could recommend only one book to busy young moms, this would be it."

—Elizabeth, former elementary school teacher and mother of two toddlers

"The section of *Queen Mom* that really spoke to me said I could quit comparing my kingdom to those around me. Satan loves to discourage us, and this is one of his tactics! But God's plan is different for each household. This book is a great read, no matter what stage of child rearing you're in."

—Cheryl, mother of four teens

"I used to wonder how I'd ever have any wits left to deal with my kids when they reached the teen years. But Brenda's honesty and practical guidelines in *Queen Mom* have given me the tools I need to deal with the stage I'm currently in. And now I can approach the future years with courage and confident parenting. I needed this book!"

—Amy, writer and mother of two elementary-age kids

"Brenda's down-to-earth style and humor help me not to lose hope while dealing with the daunting task of raising my son in a godly fashion. The ideas in *Queen Mom* lead me to think through my priorities and rules of conduct, and they challenge me to check everything against the Bible's solid foundation."

—Debra, director of women's ministry and mother of a teen son

and About Brenda Garrison

"Warmth and genuineness set the stage as Brenda Garrison engages audiences both large and small with her wise, original, and thoroughly entertaining speaking style and talent."
— Julie Ann Barnhill, international speaker and author of *She's Gonna Blow!*

"With humor and depth, Brenda Garrison reached each woman in our audience. She welcomed her audience into her life experiences and shaped her role as a godly woman, wife, mother, and friend to encourage us to remove our own masks of what a stay-at-home mom or Christian looks like. She drew us closer to grace and allowed us to examine ourselves through the transparency of her own life. To say that she was enjoyed would be an understatement."
— Sarah Moon, MOPS coordinator in Peoria, Illinois

"Brenda is a wonderful teacher and storyteller. I want to learn more from her."
"Women can identify with Brenda as she observes life vulnerably and honestly."
"Brenda offers humor, insight, and hope, based on God's grace and truth."
— Retreat attendees

"Brenda is refreshing. I liked her challenge to be authentic."
"I love . . . her humor and transparency."
"I appreciate her sharing where God has brought her from. Brenda pumps you up!"
— MOPS leadership seminar attendees

Queen M♥m

brenda garrison

Queen M♥m

a royal plan for restoring
order in your home

Standard®
PUBLISHING
Bringing The Word to Life

Cincinnati, Ohio

Published by Standard Publishing, Cincinnati, Ohio
www.standardpub.com

Project editor: Lynn Lusby Pratt
Cover and interior design: Brand Navigation

ISBN 0-7847-1986-1

Library of Congress Cataloging-in-Publication Data
Garrison, Brenda, 1959-
 Queen mom : a royal plan for restoring order in your home / Brenda Garrison.
  p. cm.
  ISBN 0-7847-1986-1 (perfect bound)
 1. Households--Religious aspects--Christianity. 2. Mother and child--Religious aspects--Christianity. 3. Households--Decision making. 4. Family--Decision making. I. Title.

 BV4526.3.G38 2007
 248.8'431--dc22
 2006029594

13 12 11 10 09 08 07   9 8 7 6 5 4 3 2 1

For my incredible husband, Gene,
and our princesses—
Katie, Kelsey, and Kerry.

Special thanks to Eric, Deb, and Danielle
and to my praying ladies—
Linda, Toni, Donna, Lora, Diane F, Dede,
Deb, Crystal, Ann, and Diane Mc.

Contents

chapter one

Who Took My Crown and Scepter?

When and How Mom Got Dethroned

"Then tell your story."

My heart almost stopped. I could barely hear what my friend said next. *Tell my story! I can't do that. What will people think of me?*

The advice came matter-of-factly as my friend nudged me toward writing this book. She has great success meeting women where they are by telling her story and being transparent. Was I ready to be open enough to tell my story to thousands of fellow moms? Was this absolutely necessary? I came to realize that, yes, it was.

The more I thought about the story of my mothering career, the more I had no clue what to say. I was not one of those moms God blessed with a compliant child right off the bat just to build her mommy self-esteem. No, God knows I have a pride problem, so he gave me just what I needed—a strong-willed child . . . followed by another strong-willed child, then a nice break to catch my breath, and five years later a compliant child.

So which story would I tell?

Should I tell how Daughter One constantly challenged my husband and me and caused us to make rules for everything, because to her if there was not a boundary, then it must be permissible? Should I tell how often and how easily she got mad at me and how I responded by getting mad back at her? Should I tell about the times Daughter Two got Daughter One in trouble and I mistakenly punished Daughter One? Should I tell about the daughter who snuck around and lied and by God's grace we caught her? (God can make computers print stuff parents need to see without the parent even hitting a key. It happened. So now my kids believe me when I tell them, "God is not on your side. He is on *our* side, and he wants you to get caught.")

You're going to hear of my mothering fiascoes, challenges, and mistakes. I hope you can identify with some; maybe a few will bring a tear. And one may even cause some I've-been-there-can't-believe-she-did-that-too laughter.

Moms, we are all in the same messy predicament. (I don't know why we're afraid to let on to each other.) Take a deep breath and try to relax for the next five minutes as you read the following fairy tale.

The Kingdom ....

Once upon a time in a land closer than you might think, the king and queen had a beautiful baby boy. They cherished him and declared his birthday a national holiday. This prince was still in diapers when the king and queen discovered that soon he would have a new sibling. Excitement and anticipation swept through the kingdom. Gifts for the new royal arrived daily.

Finally, the blessed day came. The queen gave birth to a princess. Life in the kingdom couldn't have been better.

Every morning after the nanny bathed and fed the prince and the princess, she brought them into the throne room to play while the king and queen attended to royal business in the court. The prince and princess loved to be near their parents and often made the nanny tie their blankies around their necks so they could pretend to be the king and queen.

One day the nanny brought the prince and princess to the throne room before the king and queen arrived. She watched the prince and princess play. First, the prince (who was a monkey at heart) climbed onto the king's throne. The princess was not to be outdone, so she mounted the queen's throne. They looked at each other and laughed and jumped up and down. The nanny was removing them from the thrones just as the king and queen entered the room.

The queen scolded the nanny for letting the prince and princess on the thrones. How could she allow her prince and princess to do something so mischievous? The queen wanted her children to be the perfect royals. Besides, if the nanny didn't discipline them and the queen had to be in charge of her children, she feared her temper would rule.

From that day forward, whenever they had the chance, the prince and princess climbed onto the thrones and pretended to be the king and queen. Soon they were mastering their verbal skills and learned that the servants would do whatever they told them to do. Of course, the king and queen put a stop to whatever plan was in the works. This led to temper tantrums by the little royals.

"What should we do, my dear?" lamented the queen.

"I think they need some diversion," declared the king. "Let's call the royal puppeteers to perform for the children in the nursery, and we can enjoy some peace and quiet."

Situations of disobedience and defiance arose more and more often with the prince and princess. However, the kingdom was growing and so were the demands on the king and queen. They had less time and energy for the prince and princess. Many times the king and queen gave in and let the children have their way to make up for the long hours their parents were in the court.

One evening the royal family sat down to dinner. When the servants lifted the silver covers off the plates, the king and queen were surprised to see cake and ice cream.

"This must be a mistake. Take the dessert back and bring in the entrée at once!" ordered the king.

The servant realized he had been tricked and said, "The prince and princess told us you requested cake and ice cream for dinner."

"Children," said the horrified queen, "you know we must have dinner before dessert."

"NO! NO!" objected the little royals.

The king and queen didn't want a scene. "One time won't hurt," they rationalized. So they conceded, and the family ate only cake and ice cream that evening.

Score one more for the prince and princess.

Time passed, and the kingdom flourished under the king and queen's reign. The years had gone so quickly, it hardly seemed possible that the prince would soon turn thirteen. The kingdom made preparations for the spectacular celebration.

The special evening climaxed when the king and queen bestowed a crown on the prince. "You are almost a man, son," they proclaimed. "This crown symbolizes the new responsibilities and privileges you will now have in this exciting time of your life."

Everyone oohed and aahed as the brilliant crown was placed on the prince's head. That night the prince went to bed with ideas of grandeur filling his dreams.

Across the hall in her bedroom, the princess formed a plan of her own. If the prince was getting new privileges, why shouldn't she? Everyone knows girls mature faster than boys, so in girl-years she was as mature as the prince. She should have a crown of her own too.

The next morning a storm rolled in. The castle was damp and dark, so the king and queen slept in. After a leisurely breakfast, they made their way to the throne room. They stopped cold in their tracks when they saw what was taking place.

The prince and princess were sitting on the thrones. This time they weren't pretending to be the king and queen; they were running the court. They were giving orders to the cook, the gardener, the chambermaids, the knights, and anyone else they could find. The court was in chaos.

The king and queen approached their thrones. "Children, you need to step down and let us rule the kingdom."

The prince and princess acknowledged their parents with looks that said "Make us." The prince rose from the throne, picked up the gauntlet he had been saving for just this moment, and threw it at the feet of his father. Then the prince and princess laughed in their faces.

The king and queen stared in disbelief. How did this happen? What would they do now? The prince and princess were not good at obeying them. The king and queen didn't want to make the prince and princess angry. They wanted the prince and princess to always like them. They could take away privileges, but that seemed mean. They could ground the prince and princess, but then they would have to stay home and spend time with them. Other kings and queens didn't spend time at home with their children. What would people think of the king and queen if they missed the upcoming ball so they could stay at home with their children?

They decided that the best way to keep peace in their kingdom would be to give the prince and princess whatever they desired. The *king and queen would do whatever they asked. Surely the prince and princess would eventually get tired of all this, and the king and queen would get their thrones back.*

And this is where the fairy tale becomes grim. . . .

• •

Sound like anyone you know? I want to know when the rules changed and who changed them. When and how did the Queen Mom get dethroned? Who decided the prince and princess could reign sovereign?

Reviewing the Basics

Moms, it's time we take back what God gave to us—the role of the mom. The sad truth is that in more and more homes, moms are at the beck and call of the kids. The children dictate what they are allowed to do, how they talk (even with disrespect), where they go, what they watch and listen to, and whatever else their little hearts desire. Moms are shrinking from their God-given roles and responsibilities.

And God *has* given this responsibility to us—"she watches over the affairs of her household" (Proverbs 31:27). The Bible has much to say about a mother's role. Proverbs 1:8 says, "Listen, my son, to your father's instruction and do not forsake your mother's teaching." Matthew Henry comments, "[Solomon] takes it for granted that parents will, with all the wisdom they have, instruct their children, and with all the authority they have, give law to them for their good." And "the divine law secures the honour of the mother also."[1]

It's a sobering truth: the king and queen *need* to be responsible for the well-being of the prince and princess. The Bible lays out the benefits of parental discipline: a life not cut short by bad choices; wisdom—the ability to make good decisions; saved from consequences of poor choices, including Hell; blessings, honor, and peace for the parents (Proverbs 19:18; 22:15; 29:15, 17).

God has given this responsibility to us— "she watches over the affairs of her household."

Parents need to be parents if the kids are to grow into happy, well-adjusted, and mature adults; then they will be ready to be kings and queens of their own kingdoms someday. We all know that strong kingdoms (families) make a strong nation, but in today's society we are seeing the devastating results of children growing up in weak families or without real families.

So What Happened?

Let's back up to the beginning of my own story. It too started like a fairy tale. Two love-struck redheads got married. It was a match made in Heaven. With our heads still in the clouds, we naively decided to have a little redhead of our own. *What's the big deal about having a baby?* My parents had made parenting look easy. My husband, Gene, had a totally different childhood from mine. He and his twin brother experienced chaos in their early years of childhood, so when they finally settled in a loving, stable home, it didn't even cross Gene's mind to break the rules.

What was the big deal about being parents? We were about to find out.

As I said, Princess One was born a strong-willed child (with lots of curly red hair). Just like the prince and princess in our fairy tale, she tried our patience and wisdom those first few years. Princess One didn't like to sleep, even as an infant. She took half-hour naps in her swing—one in the morning and one in the afternoon. That was it. When she hit toddlerhood, we didn't need to waste money on toys for her; she didn't play with them. She was constantly on the run. I couldn't turn my back on her, even for a second, or she would be into something. One week I had to call the poison control center twice. I'm glad they didn't have caller ID back then!

However, we kept our wits about us and stayed on our thrones. Then Princess One hit preadolescence. She developed wisdom beyond her years, knew more than we did, and definitely deserved to rule. (Do you detect a bit of sarcasm?) At least this was the fairy tale taking place in her creative mind. Combine these delusions of grandeur with her strong-willed personality—and the fact that our princess was dealing with friends who had turned into their own kind of monsters—and you can imagine the turmoil we had in our home every day. When Princess One was in the house, things were roaring.

> One week I had to call the poison control center twice. I'm glad they didn't have caller ID back then!

Princess One isn't the only one who played a part in her attempted takeover. I was unprepared for these changes, and I handled myself poorly. I too am a firstborn. I too like to be in charge. (I call it strong leadership skills; some people call it bossy.) In my family of origin, we kids didn't push the powers-that-be (Mom) very far or when the power-that-was (Dad) got home, we would be reminded of who was really in charge.

So I thought if I was firm (OK, bossy and controlling), Princess One would obey. I was firm about everything. Princess

One didn't have much breathing room, but she was wired to need breathing room. This style of parenting frustrated her, which brought on anger that she didn't know what to do with. I was missing the main idea of being a mom, which is to raise my child to be the person God designed her to be, not what I thought she should be (Proverbs 22:6).

I prayed—sometimes in spontaneous desperation and other times when I had the strength to pray with intention.

The battle lines were drawn. Strong-willed, know-it-all daughter vs. strong-willed, know-it-all mom. Oh yeah, things were getting interesting.

I cried often. I prayed—sometimes in spontaneous desperation and other times when I had the strength to pray with intention. Some days I truly wanted to run away from home. What kind of mom can't even get along with her own kid? Then I felt worse. What kind of mom even *thinks* about running away from home? I was definitely not the mom who had it all together. I was broken because our relationship was rocky. My friends were loving this time in their kids' lives. I was not loving it. I was barely surviving it.

As time went on and our relationship did not improve, the guilt strapped on my back got heavier. *What if I cause Princess One to harden her heart against the family? Or worse, against God? What if she tries something crazy? What if she turns from us and runs in the opposite direction? What if . . . ?* I felt like we were walking a tightrope with her. We couldn't give in to her demands, yet what we were doing was definitely not working. No, Princess One wasn't dethroning me on her own. My anger and frustration kept me from thinking clearly and being an effective mom. I was beating *myself* at this mom business.

Let me clearly state that we moms need to reclaim the throne!

I prayed and cried some more. I listened to the experts and read their books. Although this helped some, God finally got *his* message through to me: the core of my parenting tactics needed to change.

With an open mind I prayed for what God would show me now. I listened to him, and through a variety of ways, he showed me how to be the Queen Mom, not just for Princess One but for Princesses Two and Three as well. By trial and a lot of error, reading, and listening—to the Lord, his Word, the experts, and some wise moms—I've learned a few guidelines that have helped me be the Queen Mom that my family needs. We'll get to all that. But for starters, let me clearly state that we moms need to reclaim the throne!

Reclaiming the Throne

Preadolescence is a most difficult and crucial point in a child's life. Many moms become overwhelmed, tired, and clueless about what to do next with their preadolescent kids. So we back away, throw our hands in the air, and say, "I've done all I can do; she's in the Lord's hands now." It was at this time I read some priceless words by Joe White in *Parents' Guide to the Spiritual Mentoring of Teens:* "Now is not the time to coast. . . . You still have to play the fourth quarter—your child's teen years. . . . The final quarter of your parenting career can be your finest hour—or it can be the time when you see everything you have worked for come undone."[2]

So don't believe those lies that say moms are not important and effective. Moms *do* matter. We do make a difference, but we can't do our job from the sidelines. We need to be in the game—in our children's lives. Giving up and getting lazy is not an option.

The Bible gives us some encouragement for this time of life: "Let us throw off everything that hinders and the sin that so easily entangles, and let us run with perseverance the race marked out for us" (Hebrews 12:1). If you are a mom, the race marked out for you is the task of seeing your child through to the end.

Throw Off Busyness

So moms, how did we get off track? One answer is, we're just too busy.

The past thirty years in our American culture have been about women being "liberated" and "finding themselves." And while some of this was necessary and not all bad, society has gone from one extreme (women chained to the house) to the other (women trying to fulfill their own needs at all costs). The problem is that moms are having a hard time finding balance between spreading their wings and being the Queen Moms their families so desperately need.

Up until about thirty years ago, a mom's main responsibilities were her family, home, and perhaps a once-a-month meeting. Today's moms are trying to find time for their husbands, children, work, volunteering—and themselves. Moms are told they can (and often implied, *must*) have all the balls in the air at once and keep juggling them there perfectly. We've come to believe that since everyone else is doing *it* and the media keeps telling us to do *it,* we must do *it* too, or we will be missing out on who knows what. We are being sold a bill of goods that says we can have it all and we can have it all *now.* How insane is that?

Ecclesiastes 3:1 states, "There is a time for everything, and a season for every activity under heaven." If we have children at home, this is our season to concentrate on being the best moms God designed us to be. We get only one chance to raise each child. None of us wants to blow it, especially on things that won't matter in the big picture. This doesn't mean that we can't have a job, ministry, hobbies, and friends, but it all needs to be done with our kids' interests considered first. We will talk more about this in chapter 2.

Moms are discovering that keeping all the balls in the air takes a lot of energy. We are tired, stressed, hurried, and overwhelmed. We know we are flailing, and that causes us to feel guilty.

 We are being sold a bill of goods that says we can have it all and we can have it all <u>now.</u>

The busyness and demands of our fast-paced lives take our sights off what is really important. Our kids become just one more responsibility, another thing to check off the to-do list. Instead, they should be the love of our hearts. What is best for them should drive our decisions.

Picture this: You are standing in your front yard talking with your neighbor. You glance toward the street just in time to see an oncoming car headed for your young child who is riding her bike. Now, do you politely excuse yourself from the conversation and then saunter to the street to rescue your darling? Of course not! The split second you see the impending danger, you shift into what I call mama tiger mode—darting toward your child with lightning speed, ready to defend her at all costs. I don't know a healthy mom who would not do this for her child. Yet when it comes to everyday life, our kids and our relationships with them are easily sacrificed. We put them on hold while we meet the expectations of others.

We are too busy, tired, and distracted. That makes it easy for our little royals to sneak onto the throne and rule like tyrants.

How sad this is since, second only to our relationship with God, our children (along with our husbands, if we are married) are the most valuable parts of our lives. Our lives should reflect that. I feel like Paul felt in 1 Corinthians 9:16 when he said, "I am compelled to preach." God did an indescribable thing in me when I gave birth to my first princess, and it compels me to be a mom—though many times I fail and don't have a clue what to do next.

The world has succeeded in chipping away at the call God gave to moms. We are too busy, tired, and distracted. That makes it easy for our little royals to sneak onto the throne and rule like tyrants.

Throw Off Timidity

Maybe you haven't been dethroned due to busyness and distraction. Maybe the reason you aren't enjoying your role as the Queen Mom is because you are a bit timid about raising those kids God gave you. Their personalities are nothing like yours, and you have no idea how to deal with their disobedience, bad attitudes, and defiance. God gave those kids to you for a purpose—a purpose he wants to work *in you* and a purpose he wants to work through you *in those kids.* Together we will look at how to find that purpose and help make it a reality in your life. I hope you pick up Queen Mom confidence as we go along.

God's Way

Stop and think—what kind of mom does God want you to be? What kind of home life does God desire for your family?

God <u>did</u> make me the mom for my girls. Since that is true, God must have a way for me to be a better mom.

I hope by now your shoulders aren't drooping too low, but for your sake and your kids' sakes, keep reading. I do know how you feel. I have cried myself dry wondering why God made me a mom. I didn't feel that I was very good at it, nor did I have the "mommy touch" that some gals naturally have. But at those times I had to admit the truth: God *did* make me the mom for my girls. Since that is true, God must have a way for me to be a better mom.

God *does* have a better way. But I had to quit feeling sorry for myself and get rid of the defeatist attitude. God can't teach us anything when we focus on our pathetic little selves. I came to realize that when I'm throwing a pity party, there is room for only me—not God and not my family. Oswald Chambers observed, "No sin is worse than the sin of self-pity, because it obliterates God and puts self-interest upon the throne."[3]

No more self-pity.

Now that God had my attention, I was teachable. So what if I'd lost my crown and scepter? God could fix that. I opened up to what God was trying to show me and to the changes he wanted to make, not only in my parenting style but also in *me*. The Bible tells me that he can make these changes in me and in my mothering: "Whatever I have, wherever I am, I can make it through anything in the One who makes me who I am" (Philippians 4:13, *The Message*).

Then I had to learn the importance of patience—in dealing with myself, my kids, and my current situation. Have patience. Everything can't change overnight.

• •

My kids are teens. But the guidelines in this book are not just for parents of preteens and teenagers; they are essential and practical for raising kids of all ages. If I had clued in on them sooner, Princess One's early teen years would have been less painful for everyone in our kingdom.

Royal Decree

I want to assure you that I have not arrived. In fact, only two days ago I had one of those I-want-to-run-away-from-home moments. But moms, each of us can get back on the throne and rule as the Queen Mom was destined to do. Let's do it together.

Royal Inquiry

1. If you were to tell your own Queen Mom story ten, fifteen, or eighteen years from now, what would you hope to be able to say?

2. Recalling Hebrews 12:1, think of a "sin that so easily entangles" you personally. This sin is a huge obstacle in your parenting. Will you repent and give it to God? Find some examples and verses in the Bible that address it. If you are unfamiliar with the Bible, ask a trusted friend to help you.

3. We are to honor our parents. Just as we try to do our best, they did the best they could with what they knew. Yet we all make mistakes. What wrong tapes from your parents or your past do you play over and over—giving them another chance to harm you as you live them out daily? This may be sensitive material, but examining it will be helpful in evaluating your parenting philosophy, motives, and guidelines to see what is in line with God's Word and what is not.

4. Here are a few examples of parenting practices you may have that need to be rethought. Does your household operate under any of the following:

👑 Rules without reason (about clothes, music, hair)?

👑 Fears, either real or imagined? Fear is not from God (2 Timothy 1:7; 1 John 4:18). Pray about the issue. Give your kids to God. This doesn't discount using your brain, but don't let fear be the driving force in your parenting.

👑 Unreasonable expectations? It's possible to have unreasonable expectations for our children of all ages—even babies.

5. Have you been feeling sorry for yourself? How could a renewed effort to make God your king help your attitude?

chapter two

Peace and Order in the Kingdom

Hope for Flailing Moms

The king and queen stared in disbelief. How did this happen? What would they do now?

Many of us stare in disbelief at the messy state of our family situations. How did this happen? What *will* we do now? A book title by Robert Shaw recently caught my attention. It perfectly sums up the current condition of many families—*The Epidemic: The Rot of American Culture, Absentee and Permissive Parenting, and the Resulting Plague of Joyless, Selfish Children.* Doesn't that title say it all? Our culture is rotten, and absentee and permissive parents are letting their kids feed on it—resulting in joyless and selfish kids who are never happy or satisfied.

But moms, we can change the directions of our families— steering them toward God and his plan for them. Dr. Phil McGraw gives this advice: "In this dance of life, the question you have to ask yourself is, 'What kind of choreographer are you being?' What are you introducing into your child's life, and what are you omitting by not being plugged in? It takes focus.

What I'm asking you to do is sit down at least once a week, in a quiet moment, and assess whether or not you have a plan."[1] I suggest that we make our plan now with God and then weekly assess (with God) whether we are working our plan.

Start as if today were the first day for your family. How do you think God dreams your family to be? What characteristics and values does God want your kids to have? I'm not talking careers, lifestyle, education, or appearance, even though all of these will be affected by your kids' values. I'm talking about what makes up the real person. Who is each small child behind the stubbornness and tantrums? And what is each teen—under the layers of eye makeup, the crazy hair, the "biker Mike" jewelry, and the occasional grunt?

Whether you realize it or not, you have guiding principles that you use every day as the basis for your parenting decisions. It's important to have principles from God's Word—kingdom principles—that will get you and your family on track with his plans for all of you and will help get you, the Queen Mom, back on the throne.

Here are some big-picture, biblical principles that my husband, Gene, and I follow, along with examples of how we implement them. Get ready to start restoring peace and order in your castle!

My Family Must Come First

Unless we put our families first, we will not be successful in loving, caring for, teaching, disciplining, and enjoying our kids as God intended. The family is one of the three institutions ordained by God (the other two being the church and the government). God has established the family as the major classroom for life.

Focus on the Family's guiding principles say it best: "The family exists to propagate the race and to provide a safe and secure haven in which to nurture, teach and love the younger generation."[2] The Bible tells us, "These words which I command you today shall be in your heart; you shall teach them diligently to your children, and shall talk of them when you sit in your house, when you walk by the way, when you lie down, and when you rise up. You shall bind them as a sign on your hand, and they shall be as frontlets between your eyes. You shall write them on the doorposts of your house and on your gates" (Deuteronomy 6:6-9, *NKJV*).

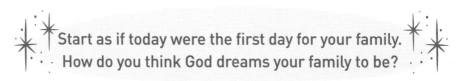

Start as if today were the first day for your family. How do you think God dreams your family to be?

These instructions from God cover every area of family life—when we are hanging out at home, when we're out in public (running errands, attending kids' activities, vacationing with friends, eating out), when we put the kids to bed, and when we get up in the morning. Every part of family life is an opportunity to teach God's Word to our kids. We can't do this if we let other things take precedence over our families.

If God has commanded us to use every part of life as an opportunity to teach our kids about him and his Word, he must know something that we have overlooked. Children listen to their moms. Look at the importance Paul placed on Timothy's mother and grandmother for his understanding of the Scriptures and subsequent salvation (2 Timothy 1:5; 3:15). Proverbs 31:10-31 is a divine word about a woman who took seriously her role as the Queen Mom—using her role and home to teach God's Word to her children. (Perhaps this is King Solomon describing his own mother.) We have a huge opportunity and responsibility to teach our children within the framework of our families.

Provide a Loving and Caring Environment

This principle comes from Jesus' words: "'Love the Lord your God with all your heart and with all your soul and with all your mind.' This is the first and greatest commandment. And the second is like it: 'Love your neighbor as yourself.' All the Law and the Prophets hang on these two commandments" (Matthew 22:37-40).

Loving God

Gene and I live lives that show the kids we love God. We're nowhere near perfect, but we try to make our decisions and choices according to our love and devotion to God. Part of showing our love for God is making time with him a priority—both individually and corporately.

Standard Publishing recommends these books that are designed to bring kids closer to God:

Young children—My Favorite Verses series by Dandi Daley Mackall, The NLT® Story Bible Series developed with Dr. Mary Manz Simon, *Don't Mess with Moses!* by Marty Nystrom

Tweens—*365 Trivia Twist Devotions* by Betsy Schmitt and Dave Veerman, *Through the Bible Devotions* by Mark Littleton, *Me and My God* by Joy Stevans

Teens—*Astonishing Tales of Spiritual Truth* by Steven James, *Devotions by Dead People* by Lynn Lusby Pratt, *Green's Not Your Best Color* by Mieka Phillips

For our girls to know and love God, they need to know how to have a personal quiet time. Then they need to do it. I give my girls the tools they need to meet with God. At Anne Graham Lotz's *Just Give Me Jesus* revival, I learned a great way to study God's Word. I typed out the plan and gave each daughter a copy. Now they have a way to study the Bible that will take them through life as they mature into beautiful Christian women. A devotional book or other inspirational material is almost crucial for guiding them into God's presence. (For our teen girls, we love *Brio* and *Brio and Beyond* magazines from Focus on the Family.)

At any inspired time I may give them a Bible verse and thought on an index card. It may be something they need to hear (I'm sure they love this!), or it may be something *I* need to hear (but they don't know that!). I don't talk about it or preach. I just place it on their beds and let the Holy Spirit speak.

The second aspect of time with God consists of spending time with him as a family. In Deuteronomy 4:9, Moses challenged Israel, "Be careful, and watch yourselves closely so that you do not forget the things your eyes have seen or let them slip from your heart as long as you live. Teach them to your children and to their children after them." We do this in two ways.

Every evening before bed we have a prayer time together. Some of my friends have given me the you-gotta-be-kidding look when I let it slip that we do this. The topic of family devotions of any kind is an area of frustration and guilt for most Christian families. I believe that is because we often set our sights on an unrealistic goal. A casual, *brief* prayer time before bedtime works for us. At times some of us have come to it discouraged, tired, and at odds with each other, yet we have done it anyway. It forces us to soften our hearts toward God and each other. Gene and I share with the kids examples of how God is faithful in providing for us and guiding us. We help them see how he is doing the same in their lives.

Going to church as a family also grows our family spiritually, and it shows the kids the importance of worshiping with other believers. We are taught the Word and learn to respect God (Deuteronomy 31:12, 13), and we get to know other Christians. The only time the kids may be excused is after a rare late night (getting home late from a competition or prom) and of course, for sickness.

Loving and Caring for Each Other

Jesus said that the second greatest commandment is "Love your neighbor as yourself." Our families are our closest neighbors, so they are the ones we should love and care for first. Family is the training field where we learn to think about and serve someone other than self. This is accomplished by each member looking to the needs of the others first (Philippians 2:3, 4). Being part of a family meets one of our most basic needs—to belong. Kids especially feel this need, so most will find a way to belong *somewhere.* Why else do kids flock to cliques, sports teams (even if they don't get to play), bands, and even gangs (despite the negative consequences they may have to bear)? They want to belong. Let's give them a better place to belong—their families!

Respect Is Not an Option

Respect is a huge issue in our society, especially in our schools. An article in *Parade* magazine makes the case for our children's needing to show respect: "A new study from the nonpartisan group Public Agenda found that 34% of America's teachers have considered quitting because discipline has broken down." The teachers tell it straight as the article continues, "Middle and high school teachers say kids don't learn discipline at home. 'There's disrespect everywhere in our culture,' notes one teacher. 'Students absorb it and bring it to school.'"[3]

Moms, these are our kids, and we need to wake up to reality. Lack of respect is rampant, yet the Bible tells us that we are not to live that way: "Show proper respect to everyone" (1 Peter 2:17).

I have almost dropped my teeth on the many occasions I have heard teenagers rudely chastise their mothers for one thing or another—followed by the moms offering an apology for not living up to their children's expectations. Excuse me—who *is* the parent here? I have been just as shocked when I have seen a small child take a swipe at his mom (not hitting hard enough to hurt but definitely sending the message of defiance), and the mom laughed as if this were cute, childish behavior.

At these times I've felt like screaming "Who's in charge?!" Moms, we can't ignore these red flags of disrespect. Dennis Rainey, president and cofounder of FamilyLife, agrees: "We've swung too far in the opposite direction when we allow our teenagers [*I would add "young children"*] to show disrespect at the expense of adults without being disciplined and corrected."[4] If our kids get by with it now, they will continue to be disrespectful to everyone, including God.

God has some strong words about respect. He commands us to respect him and tells us that benefits result. Respecting God teaches wisdom (Psalm 111:10), adds length to life (Proverbs 10:27), helps us avoid evil (Proverbs 16:6), and leads to life and peace (Proverbs 19:23).

 I've felt like screaming "Who's in charge?!"

Parents teach kids respect by first showing it themselves. We show respect to God by loving him and living according to his Word (Deuteronomy 6:13). We show respect by talking to each other with respect. Each person may express his or her feelings and thoughts as long as it is done appropriately—personal attacks are not allowed.

Respect is also shown by not getting into each other's stuff or personal space without permission. Teach your children to knock and request entrance into someone's room. A shut bathroom door means someone wants privacy, and that should be honored (unless the occupant is a four-year-old giving himself a haircut!). It is appropriate for a parent to knock and ask if everything is OK, but it is inappropriate for anyone (parent or sibling) to barge in. Consideration helps build a sense of security and respect in the family.

Relationships Are a Priority

We start with the couple's relationship. In Genesis 2:24 God instituted marriage, so we need to keep our marriages strong. This is done by putting the marriage relationship first. When kids see their parents loving each other and committed to each other, it gives the kids a sense of security.

Every evening after dinner, before the dishes are done, Gene and I go on a date—no kids allowed. We walk for two miles. We talk about the day, whine a little, and encourage each other. Sometimes we may get into an argument, and since we are alone for thirty minutes, it is usually resolved by the time we get home. This date time works for us, but it probably won't work for every couple, so be creative in making time to be with each other.

  Every evening after dinner, before the dishes are done, Gene and I go on a date—no kids allowed.

Our best friends, Tom and Denise, spend a lot of time apart during the week because of Tom's travel schedule. So they do some things to keep their marriage strong. Every night Tom is away, he calls Denise at nine o'clock and they talk about their days. Once a year, after a year's time of traveling, he has accumulated enough frequent flier points to enable them to take a nice trip without the children. Strong marriages support strong families, so put this relationship first.

Then, the most basic place to start building family relationships is at the dining table—whether it is breakfast or dinner. OK, you moms of older (and maybe overinvolved) kids who just threw your hands in the air and gave up . . . breathe. At this moment you don't have to figure out how to do this; just think about it. Is this a value you want for your family—the whole family eating together most days?

This is such a no-brainer that Hollywood has even figured it out. TV stars (many of whom seem to have little or no family values) are doing public service announcements telling us the benefits of eating dinner together as a family. Our society has taken away from us this basic building block of family life; now we have to relearn mealtime.

Pay attention—this is how it's done: Set the table with real dishes. Put food (either homemade, from the freezer, or take-out) on the table. Call every member of the family to the table. No TV, no radio, no newspaper, no cell phones, no computer games, no PDAs, no MP3s, and no excuses. Just your family and food. Ask someone to say a prayer. Then eat and talk to each other (of course, not with food in your mouth!). The benefits are numerous and far-reaching.

The National Center on Addiction and Substance Abuse (CASA) at Columbia University has consistently found that "the more often children eat dinner with their families the less likely they are to smoke, drink or use illegal drugs." In response to this research, a national effort, Family Day—A Day to Eat Dinner with Your Children, is being launched to "promote parental engagement [in children's lives] as a simple, effective way to reduce substance abuse by children and teens and raise healthier children."[5]

Isn't it ridiculous that we now need "experts" to tell us what our moms and grandmothers knew? Doesn't it stand to reason that if dining with our kids helps steer them away from smoking, drinking, and drugs, those mealtimes can have a positive effect in other areas of their lives? And isn't that what we want?

Another benefit of eating meals together is that magically, without any manipulation on your part, bonds are formed between family members. Sure, there will be rough spots—arguments, unkind words, rebellious attitudes—but the table is the place for all that to be worked through. There will also be laughter, compassion, and cheering each other on. This is what family is all about—teaching kids about life and helping them mature within the loving, safe environment called home.

> **Isn't it ridiculous that we now need "experts" to tell us what our moms and grandmothers knew?**

If eating meals together seems like the Land of Oz to your family, start thinking about it . . . and the benefits. Pray for God to change your heart, to work in your family members' hearts and schedules, and to get everyone to the table together. Yes, it will require work on your part too, and you probably will take grief for it, but you are the queen. You can do this.

If you're a Queen Mom of little ones, your family may all be together for dinner every night. But do the children stay at the table for a little conversation, or have you trained them to get down as soon as they are done eating? Even the smallest child can be taught to sit in his chair for a few minutes and contribute to the conversation. This teaches children to be part of the family, and it counteracts a me-first mentality.

To keep relationships strong and healthy, we must make sure family relationships take precedence over relationships with others. This does not mean that you or your children abandon a social life. It *does* mean that the needs of the family come first.

Gene and I are rarely away from home in the evening because we know it is important to be there interacting with the girls. Recently I was vividly reminded of how necessary it is for me to be home for the girls. I returned from an overnight speaking engagement to learn that our youngest had had a first-time, huge fight with her best friend. Even more interesting, this little friend's mom is my best friend. She called to ask if I knew what was going on with the girls, but since I hadn't been home, I had no clue.

That evening was full of talking, counseling, crying, and praying with Princess Three. The issue was resolved. Princesses One and Two had issues of their own that evening that needed the queen's attention. My girls are not wimpy crybabies; however, having Mom's listening ear keeps them on an even keel.

Sure, Gene and I take time for our friends; but at this point in our lives, we give the majority of our time to the girls. We have realized that they won't always be living under our roof.

Another way we keep the family ties strong is by attending each other's functions. Kerry is seven years younger than Katie and five years younger than Kelsey, so she has sat through innumerable band and chorus performances, Christmas programs, and school plays. Now it is Kerry's turn, and even though Katie and Kelsey would rather be on a date or even doing homework, they *will* be in the audience cheering for their sister.

Work Makes Fun FUN

My kids have heard this so many times that they have it memorized. While it's true, there is more value in work than that. Teaching our kids how to work and the value of a job well done is part of our job. God is our example. He made all that exists (Genesis 1, 2). The Old Testament is full of examples of people who worked hard to accomplish God's plan: Noah built the ark (Genesis 6:13-22), Solomon led Israel in building the temple (1 Kings 5, 6), Nehemiah and the returned exiles rebuilt the wall around Jerusalem (Nehemiah 1–6). In 1 Thessalonians 4:11, 12, the apostle Paul tells us that doing our work is part of our good example to the world.

Working together to take care of the home and each other teaches kids that they belong and are part of something bigger than themselves.

Doing chores as a family has many purposes. Working together to take care of the home and each other teaches kids that they belong and are part of something bigger than themselves. They learn the value of work, how to work, and some necessary life skills.

A Good Work Ethic

I want my girls not to be afraid to work. The Bible gives the best definition of a good work ethic and the motive for it: "Whatever you do, work at it with all your heart, as working for the Lord, not for men, since you know that you will receive an inheritance from the Lord as a reward. It is the Lord Christ you are serving" (Colossians 3:23, 24). Wow! This is a better incentive than the allowance we give the girls! Having a good work ethic will be invaluable to them when they get to the real work world and even when they have their own homes.

> "Whatever you do, work at it with all your heart, as working for the Lord."

Part of our training includes daily chores and Saturday morning housecleaning. I have taught them how to clean each room, scrub floors, and clean toilets. Since I want them to make the best use of their time and enjoy the rest of the day, the rule is that the work needs to be done by noon. When they are finished, I inspect their work. Quality control.

Basic Life Skills

The principle of teaching basic life skills is strongly and clearly stated in Titus 2:4, 5: "[The older women] can train the younger women to love their husbands and children, to be self-controlled and pure, to be busy at home, to be kind, and to be subject to their husbands, so that no one will malign the word of God."

This does not mean that our girls are to be chained to their future homes (see Proverbs 31:10-31 for the description of a well-balanced woman). It *does* mean that their homes and families will come before careers, friends, and volunteering—and they need to learn how to care for them.

We work on cooking skills when the girls' schedules are not so busy (Christmas vacation and long weekends). One of the girls cooks a meal. I am there to help and guide, but she does the work. Now the oldest two have basic culinary skills to build on. Hey, we all need to eat. How do we think our daughters will feed their families if we don't teach them to cook?

I love to sew, and I did my best to pass that affection on to my girls. But it didn't take—they have other interests. However, they did learn their way around a needle, thread, and sewing machine. What more can a queen ask?

Gene has taught them how to mow the grass, put gas in the car, check its oil, and when to get the oil changed. Once I destroyed a car because I did not check the oil. It was an expensive lesson. If we don't teach our kids how to live in the real world, how will they learn?

Kids learn how to do life from their dads and moms, and that takes time together doing the everyday stuff.

Kids learn how to do life from their dads and moms, and that takes time together doing the everyday stuff. I want my kids to be honest, selfless, hardworking, kind, responsible, confident, and respectful. My desire is that they see Gene and me living this way when doing business at the store, caring for the family, in our finances, when dealing with difficult people, when circumstances change for the worse . . . Then they'll catch it and live it out (Deuteronomy 6:6-9).

Teach Responsibility

God calls us to be responsible in every area of our lives. In Luke 16 Jesus told the story of the rich man and his lazy household manager. The manager was accused of "wasting [the rich man's] possessions" (v. 1). As with many lazy people, he was not stupid. The manager got his brain in gear and devised a plan to save himself from physical labor in the event that he lost his job. His equally wicked boss—the rich man—applauded his craftiness. (Jesus doesn't say whether the manager kept his job.)

Jesus teaches the point: "Whoever can be trusted with very little can also be trusted with much, and whoever is dishonest with very little will also be dishonest with much" (v. 10).

The lesson to us is, God owns it all (Psalm 50:10). We are just the managers of what he has given us to handle. This means everything that comes to us. Yes, money, but much more—time, talents, relationships, education, career, family . . . everything. Unreliability is not an attribute that reflects Christ in us. We need to be responsible in all areas and teach our children to do the same.

Financial Responsibility

This is a worthy goal for our kids. Financial responsibility includes living within their budgets and learning to save, while also spending some of their money on things they want and sometimes need. Maybe you have shied away from teaching on these matters because *you* are not financially responsible. But remember, how can God trust you with more if you are not faithful in what you have?

Let me briefly describe how we teach financial responsibility to our princesses. Each princess gets an allowance according to her age. That money is divided into four categories:

For God—to be spent how they choose—for missionaries, Christian radio, VBS . . .

For savings—to be spent on an item that is planned for. This summer Kerry outgrew her bike. She decided she didn't want a hand-me-down. She wanted to use her money to buy a new bike, and that is just what she did. She loves riding this bike because she paid for it herself with the money she saved for weeks. I don't recommend indefinite saving—that is discouraging for kids because they see no results, and it teaches them to hoard.

For spending—to be used for their entertainment or a fun item they want. When our girls go out with friends, we don't hand them money and tell them to have fun. We tell them to have fun with their money. It is amazing how discerning they are when they are spending their own money. One of our princesses became very picky about the shampoo and other toiletries she wanted. We began making her buy these pricey items with her own money. She eventually became less particular.

For gifts—to be spent on whatever gifts they buy. This is another area in which the girls have become more thoughtful about their spending choices. They are choosier about the price of gifts for friends when they are shelling out the bucks. It also gives the kids the pleasure of giving. This year for Gene's birthday, Kerry used all her gift money to buy her dad a pair of denim shorts that were cool; Dad's other shorts were just "too dorky." Kerry is seeing how financial responsibility pays off. She had her money to use and fully enjoyed doing so.

It is amazing how discerning they are when they are spending their own money.

Just think how happy our future sons-in-law will be with wives who are financially self-disciplined!

Personal Responsibility

This is necessary for kids to survive and thrive in the real world. The Bible is full of commands that call us to be personally responsible. Start with Proverbs 1–3, and you will find instruction on attaining wisdom, fearing God, staying out of trouble, keeping pure, being kind, being honest, trusting God . . .

Children must learn to take care of their personal affairs and carry through on what they say they will do. They can start small and work up. Are our kids faithful in the "very little" (Luke 16:10), or are they dishonest with the very little? Do they get their homework done, or do they waste time on the computer? Do they take care of their possessions, or are they careless with their things, taking it for granted that we parents will just buy new stuff?

 ## I do not pick up dirty laundry.

Do they get their laundry to the laundry room, or do they have you trained to pick it up? I do not pick up dirty laundry. Even now as I am writing, I am doing laundry. One of the precious princesses has a pile of dirty laundry in her bathroom, and that is where it will stay until she picks it up. Too bad she missed getting it washed. And no fair doing her own small load of such neglected laundry—that is a waste of water and electricity. There are just some things in life that you have to fall in line with. In the real world the boss will not move the deadline just because it is more convenient for the princess. Such life lessons are more easily learned at home.

Do your kids get themselves up, or have they trained you to get them out of bed, thereby releasing themselves of this responsibility? Our princesses are responsible for getting themselves out of bed in the morning at the time they need to be up. This mom does not remind, prod, scream at, or jump up and down on sleeping kids. Either they get up and get going, or they don't—and then *they* pay the consequences. The consequence is often reality itself—they are late, and the authority figure there gives them grief. Don't step in. Let them taste life.

One year Katie and Kelsey had jazz band practice at seven fifteen three mornings a week. Their instructor was young and new and determined to break these kids in right. If they were late he called them on the carpet for it. Let's just say they were rarely late. If their lateness affects me (i.e., I must drive them to school after they miss the bus), I give them a painful consequence (usually one of my chores) to help them remember to get moving earlier next time.

• •

Our job is to prepare our kids for life. Treating them as if they are children until they turn eighteen will only keep them children—and it will keep the kingdom in chaos.

Royal Decree

OK, what has God spoken to you about? Read again the Bible verses in this chapter. Think through my suggestions. Get something down on paper. Nothing fancy—just indicate what you are going to do to help restore peace and order. These will be the guidelines (backed by Scripture) on which you base your parenting decisions. Proverbs 22:6 doesn't guarantee we can make our children turn out a certain way, but we are responsible to do our best to train them in that way. You can do this!

Royal Inquiry

1. So what do you think God wants your family to become? Note some ideas—nothing set in stone, just a little kindling to get the fire going. This process will take thoughtful prayer (give God all your ideas, concerns, questions, and doubts—he can handle it), conversations with your husband (or a trusted friend, if you're a single parent), and some serious listening to the Lord.

2. Do you realize how important your words and actions are in showing God to your child? Consider opportunities you have to teach your kids about God—not just about him, but about experiencing him. Could you discuss with them: times when he provided for the family? times when he forgave sin (yes, even moms and dads sin)? times when you obeyed God and were blessed because of it?

3. If you believe family relationships take precedence over relationships with others, how are you demonstrating it?

4. Do your kids feel secure in your love and know how much they mean to you? What have you shown them in your attitude and daily actions? Is there anything you need to change?

chapter three

Subtle (or Not So Subtle) Insurrection

Teaching Kids the World Does Not Revolve Around Them

From that day forward, whenever they had the chance, the prince and princess climbed onto the thrones and pretended to be the king and queen. Soon they were mastering their verbal skills and learned that the servants would do whatever they told them to do.

"It's All About Me!" reads the red, metal die-cut sign in our kitchen. I didn't buy it because I believe it; I bought it to remind our princesses that "It *Isn't* All About Me!" They laughed when I hung it up; but every so often I point to the sign and gently say, "Remember, it's not all about you."

"I *know*, Mmmomm!"

Madison Avenue may think they invented the all-about-me cliché, but the sentiment was around before life was breathed into man. Satan raged, "It's all about me!" when he instigated the original insurrection against God. Adam and Eve's actions revealed they believed "It's all about me!" when they didn't trust

God and did things their way. So when our children try to take the throne and make life all about themselves, they are being true to the sinful human nature we all have.

Kids don't wait long to attempt an insurrection against the king and queen. Infants scream in the middle of the night so they can have a midnight snack and be cozily rocked back to sleep. Toddlers soon learn that even though they cannot communicate verbally, they can communicate through body language.

How crazy is it for a two-foot-tall toddler to be demanding that an adult obey?

As I sat talking with a young mom, her eighteen-month-old child stood next to her. This toddling princess wasn't happy about not having her Queen Mom's full attention. So she threw a tantrum. She stomped her tiny foot, furrowed her angelic brow, and uttered a low grunt to warn Queen Mom that more was coming unless she got her way. Her mom looked frustrated and said, "She does this when she doesn't get her way." *Oh really? I've never seen a child throw a hissy fit to get her way!* Of course, we all have seen this, and we cringe. How crazy is it for a two-foot-tall toddler to be demanding that an adult obey?

Children's attempts at insurrection aren't always as obvious as an eighteen-month-old's temper tantrum. Hints of trouble can creep in during the early school years as the kids become involved in extracurricular activities. The child becomes involved in one activity, maybe T-ball. The young parents reason, "Since she enjoyed that so much, let's enroll her in fall soccer. Wow, she's really good at sports. Let's see how she does with gymnastics."

And so begins an activities schedule that takes up all the child's time. She has no time for free play or for learning personal responsibility and life skills. As the family's life is reduced to getting this child to all her activities, she's put in prime position to begin believing that everything revolves around her.

I dread marching band season. Two of our princesses have been active in marching band. The busyness escalates from July to November. The further into the season, the more time the directors demand. The girls enjoyed being part of the band with their friends; but after September, even *they* were ready to slow down. During this time they were still responsible for their personal duties (cleaning their bedrooms, getting dirty laundry to the laundry room, doing their homework), and they tried to keep up. But many times they couldn't do their chores because band kept them busy Friday night and all day Saturday, often getting them home at midnight or later. With their midweek practice and homework, we felt as if we seldom saw them.

This year Princess Two had no break between band and her madrigal dinner rehearsals and performances. More and more, I was called upon at the last minute to take care of her responsibilities and run errands for her. This is OK once in a while, but it's not a lifestyle to be adopted.

No Time for Relationships

During band season, Princess Two gave us sporadic blurbs about who said what to whom, how she felt about the directors, and oh, did she mention she would need twenty dollars for meals on Saturday's band trip?

Princess One handled band season differently. The less she was home, the less she talked. She needed time to unwind, process her thoughts and feelings, and then share. So we barely got a grunt. And to add to our joy, since she was drum major and took comments from both sides of the podium, she often came home upset—which needed further processing, which required further time, which we didn't have because of the crazy schedule . . . I think you get the picture.

Parents can't afford *not* to be up on their teens' lives. Thankfully, this was the only time our daughters' schedules were that crazy. But many kids keep up a frenzied pace all year.

The story is the same whether the child is six or sixteen. Kids are too busy. This topic of childhood busyness could fill a book, but here I want to examine one result of it—the nurturing of kids' natural selfish tendencies.

What happens when moms and dads work their schedules around the kids' schedules? Family dinners are rare because the dinner hour is spent driving kids to their activities. Kids don't have time to learn life skills or build relationships. Their time is spent in school, the gym, the dance studio, or on the practice field. Without a word from us, our kids learn that the world revolves around them. How? Why? Because we have shown them it does.

It is not God's desire for our kids to be lazy and coddled.

Children are quick learners. It doesn't take long for them to assimilate the message we have been teaching them: "It's all about me!" They jump right into their new roles as prince and princess. No wonder this generation is full of self-centered kids. "Me" is the only person we have given them time to think about.

We can also give kids who are doing nothing the same message—that life is all about them. The temptation is strong to overindulge the child who has no interests and no ambition. Many times the parent goes overboard coddling him, trying to ignite a spark. This does not work. Look at your own experiences with your heavenly Father. How does God get you to deal with your negative behavior? Does he bless you, or does he allow difficulties to get your attention? I know I go running to God for direction when life gets uncomfortable. Often we can get our kids moving by causing some discomfort in their lives.

Taking Action

It is not God's desire for our kids to be lazy and coddled. Paul says it clearly: "Don't you remember the rule we had when we lived with you? 'If you don't work, you don't eat'" (2 Thessalonians 3:10, *The Message*). So if we want our prince to stop acting like a spoiled royal, we need to take action. Dr. James Dobson recommends letting the consequences of any negative behavior kick in.

How does one connect behavior with consequences? By being willing to let the child experience a reasonable amount of pain or inconvenience when he behaves irresponsibly. When Jack misses the school bus through his own dawdling, let him walk a mile or two and enter school in midmorning (unless safety factors prevent this). If Janie carelessly loses her lunch money, let her skip a meal. Obviously, it is possible to carry this principle too far, being harsh and inflexible with an immature child. But the best approach is to expect boys and girls to carry the responsibility that is appropriate for their age and occasionally to taste the bitter fruit that irresponsibility bears. In so doing, behavior is wedded to consequences, just like in real life.[1]

I love this consequence-matches-the-action principle in parenting. It works immensely better than nagging.

One of our princesses felt it was her right to stay in her room with the door shut and the music on so she wouldn't have to interact with the family. At dinnertime she couldn't hear the queen's announcement that dinner was being served. The other princesses had to go to her room, open the door, and tell her it was time to eat. King Gene decreed this was ridiculous. Further, if the princess wants to eat, she must keep her door open and be alert to what is going on outside her self-proclaimed territory.

I love this consequence-matches-the-action principle in parenting. It works immensely better than nagging.

So the decree immediately went into effect. It took only one time of not being called to dinner. The door is now open, and this princess is attentive to the rest of the family.

What do I most want my kids to know how to do when they are adults? Play soccer, do a back flip off the high bar, play a musical instrument, get the high score on the latest video or computer game? Or properly care for their homes, not be afraid of hard work, and develop meaningful relationships with their families, friends, and the Lord?

This does not have to be an either/or situation. Certainly there is nothing wrong with playing sports, learning a musical instrument, and having fun with friends. I'm pleased that my girls are gifted musically, because I'm tone deaf. I'm glad that they are physically coordinated to march and do their pom-pom dance routines. (I still cringe when I think of my seventh-grade cheerleading tryout!) These talents are part of who God made them to be, and they should participate and have fun. The danger comes when these events take precedence over family and home. An overly busy lifestyle keeps kids immature and self-centered. It doesn't prepare them for the fast-approaching realities of life.

> You are the Queen Mom. Act like it. You've got to know and claim the role God gave you. It may be a little crazy (or a lot crazy) in your castle right now, but you can rule.

How do we achieve that healthy balance between signing our kids up for a few well-chosen activities and showing them that the world does not revolve around them?

I Am the Queen. I Rule.

When our first two princesses were babies, their pediatrician was the same pediatrician I had gone to as a child. This doctor had been in practice for decades, and nothing surprised him. When I took the girls in because of their ear infections, they got a huge injection of penicillin—and I got a huge injection of parenting confidence. Our doctor was great at giving young parents the self-assurance needed to do the job without fretting or wringing our hands. I want to give you a huge injection of parenting confidence. Like the injection of penicillin, it may hurt a little, but it will help.

You are the Queen Mom. Act like it. You've got to know and claim the role God gave you. It may be a little crazy (or a lot crazy) in your castle right now, but you can rule.

Consider your plan for parenting—you're on the right track by reading and thinking through this book. Develop a plan and stick to it. One of our princesses is a quick thinker and debater. She can convince me I'm wrong even when I began with steeled conviction. When that happens I stop the discussion and tell her I will consult with the king. This gives me time to think things through, make any necessary changes, and get reinforcement.

  God has given us the best place to teach our kids about life and relationships—within the family.

Boys proficiently use debating tactics on their moms. My friend, Vicki, and her husband, Bob, are highly educated and bright. They produced three brainiacs. Every once in a while, their oldest son calmly drew Vicki into a debate about his latest scheme, eventually turned her will to jelly, and got his way. Bob would come home from work, quickly see that an insurrection was well underway, and intervene. Then he would gently, but firmly, remind Vicki, "You're the mom. He's the kid. Don't let him do this to you." Don't let a prince—at any age—back you into a corner with demands or debates.

It's My Job to Teach

We must teach our children how to live according to God's Word. In King Solomon's day the mom was the teacher of life's lessons for her children. "Listen, my son, to your father's instruction and do not forsake your mother's teaching" (Proverbs 1:8).

God has given us the best place to teach our kids about life and relationships—within the family. God instituted the family in Genesis 2:23, 24. His Word is full of instruction on doing family well. God valued family enough to have his Son be born into an imperfect family (like ours), to be raised from an infant to a mature, perfect man who became our sacrificial Lamb. We have been given a great trust and opportunity to raise our kids. Paul challenges us to do it well: "It is required that those who have been given a trust must prove faithful" (1 Corinthians 4:2).

In the movie *The Princess Diaries,* ordinary teenager Mia is shocked to learn from her grandmother, Queen Clarisse, that she is the Princess of Genovia. Queen Clarisse tries to convince Mia of the distinguished opportunity she has been given. She goes on to encourage Mia that she will be with her and prepare her so she can reign: "We will accept the challenge of helping you become the princess that you are." She continues, "You will study languages, history, art, political science. I can teach you to walk, talk, sit, stand, eat, dress like a princess." Queen Clarisse knows the demands that will be on her granddaughter, and she wants her well prepared to rule.

 "It is required that those who have been given a trust must prove faithful."

A great way to rid kids of the barriers of selfishness they tend to build around their little kingdoms is by working together as a family. While some of my friends pay someone to clean their houses, I prefer to call on my three cleaning ladies—Princesses One, Two, and Three. Every Saturday morning we each have one fourth of the house to clean. We finish before anyone leaves for fun with friends or does homework. Of course, exceptions are made when the occasional activity comes up. But as a rule, unless the princesses are sick, they will be cleaning house Saturday mornings.

I have serious concerns when kids (especially elementary and junior-high age) have scheduled activities much of the day Saturday and most evenings. They have no time to chip in at home. They take care of only their little worlds—if that. That mind-set won't take them very far in life.

God ordained work. He was the first one to work when he created everything. Why should our kids be exempt from work, pursuing only their desires? Working as a family leads to making a worthwhile contribution to society and to the body of Christ.

Kids get a sense of satisfaction and accomplishment when a job is well done (or even done only to their best ability), which leads to a strong sense of self-worth. Once in a while one of my girls has a friend over during a time she needs to be doing her assigned chore, and the friend often jumps in and helps. I can tell when this friend isn't used to doing work at home, because she gets such a charge out of helping and seeing the job done well.

The wise Queen Mom also knows the value of encouraging the development of relationships within her family. In our families we learn to love, to accept, to respect and honor, to laugh, to share confidences, to forgive, and to venture out and come back. This takes time, both quality and quantity.

 Kids get a sense of satisfaction and accomplishment when a job is well done (or even done only to their best ability), which leads to a strong sense of self-worth.

Our three princesses are highly social (as is their queen), so I must jealously guard our designated family times. I block out several hours when we are home doing our own things, intercepting the other person doing her thing, many times all ending up flopped on the sofas, talking and laughing. Even the all-powerful queen can't orchestrate the interaction and bonding, but she can provide the fertile atmosphere in which it can grow.

I want my princesses to put others first in friendship and service, following the example of the true royal, the King of kings, Jesus.

My girls love to watch one of their favorite movies, *Ever After*, on these lazy afternoons. It is a fresh, realistic retelling of the Cinderella story. The princess-to-be, Danielle, is kind, generous, and hardworking (humbly serving her wicked stepmother and stepsisters). She even daringly portrays herself to be a baroness in order to buy back a servant and reunite him with his wife. Of course, in the end the prince falls in love with Danielle. They are married, and she becomes the princess. All the kingdom loves her, as do the servants in the castle. Why? Because she has proven through friendship and service that she cares about them. She is worthy of their respect and adoration.

I want my princesses to put others first in friendship and service, following the example of the true royal, the King of kings, Jesus. Philippians 2:3-11 (*The Message*) articulates my desire perfectly:

Don't push your way to the front; don't sweet-talk your way to the top. Put yourself aside, and help others get ahead. Don't be obsessed with getting your own advantage. Forget yourselves long enough to lend a helping hand.

Think of yourselves the way Christ Jesus thought of himself. He had equal status with God but didn't think so much of himself that he had to cling to the advantages of that status no matter what. Not at all. When the time came, he set aside the privileges of deity and took on the status of a slave, became human! Having become human, he stayed human. It was an incredibly humbling process. He didn't claim special privileges. Instead, he lived a selfless, obedient life and then died a selfless, obedient death—and the worst kind of death at that: a crucifixion.

Because of that obedience, God lifted him high and honored him far beyond anyone or anything, ever, so that all created beings in heaven and on earth—even those long ago dead and buried—will bow in worship before this Jesus Christ, and call out in praise that he is the Master of all, to the glorious honor of God the Father.

This teaching and modeling for our kids requires one key element—time. Some things just take time:

- showing a four-year-old how to set the table
- listening to a seven-year-old girl tell about all the gross things the boys at school did during lunch
- being available when a fourteen-year-old boy decides to talk to you for ten minutes
- helping two hormonal teens understand each other
- reading between the lines and know something is not right in your child's life

The Benefits of Obedience

Take a posture now that says you want to make the time

to reign as queen. It will be so worth it. It is C
kids to have moms who do their jobs. And our
instructed to obey, respect, and honor their kir
(Ephesians 6:1-3). In Colossians 3:20 God tells (
your parents in everything, for this pleases the Lord." They can t
follow God's plan for them if we parents are running around
taking orders from them.

These calls to obedience come with benefits for our children.
In the Ephesians 6 passage, Paul tells us that obedience to
parents is right—it is how children are to live. Then he quotes
from the Ten Commandments, adding that honoring parents
brings blessing and prolonged life. He states in Colossians 3 that
obedience to parents pleases the Lord.

Don't we want our kids to have God's best? His Word shows us
that his best consists of moms doing their job (confidently ruling
on the throne) so children can do theirs (learning obedience,
respect, and honor), thereby being blessed and growing into the
mature, Christian adults God planned for them to be.

• •

Building our kingdoms is an ongoing process. But if we
do our best, we will have no regrets. If our kids turn into
mature, wise, unselfish, responsible adults who follow hard
after God, we can say it was all worth it. If they choose to
follow a different path . . . well, we know we gave them
our best. The rest is up to them and the Lord. You are the
mom. You know best. Sure, you don't know everything, but
you know a whole lot more than your kids (or their friends)
do. What you don't know, find out; get in the Word and talk
with any wise, godly mom who has a few battle scars.

ı you haven't been on the throne for a while, you may be feeling overwhelmed and hopeless right now. But that is from Satan. You know it is God's plan for you to be the Queen Mom, and you know it is best for your kids *not* to be in charge. Take a breath and acknowledge these truths. Soak in these verses for a minute: "Those who know your name trust in you, for you, O LORD, have never abandoned anyone who searches for you" (Psalm 9:10, *NLT*). "He tends his flock like a shepherd: He gathers the lambs in his arms and carries them close to his heart; he gently leads those that have young" (Isaiah 40:11). He's talking about us!

Royal Inquiry

1. Have you communicated to your child that "It's all about me"? If yes, how?

2. Has your child succeeded in making life all about him, or tried to? If yes, how?

3. What are the results on your family and your child's character?

4. What do you want your kids to know how to do when they are adults?

5. Do you believe you are the Queen Mom? If not, what is keeping you from claiming your throne?

6. Jot down two or three things you can begin to do now that will teach your kids that they are not in charge and will help them take their focus off themselves.

7. Are you willing to commit the time it will take to be the Queen Mom? Talk this over with the Lord, and let him guide you in a plan that is best for your kingdom.

chapter four

The Queen Mom Does Not Rule with an Iron Fist

Anger Management for Mom

The queen scolded the nanny for letting the prince and princess on the thrones. How could she allow her prince and princess to do something so mischievous? The queen wanted her children to be the perfect royals. Besides, if the nanny didn't discipline them and the queen had to be in charge of her children, she feared her temper would rule.

I still get sick when I remember the first time I really lost my temper with our girls. Princess One was just finishing a round of chicken pox, and Princess Two was starting her turn with the illness. They were ages five and three. I was outside trying to paint the window trim, and the girls kept running out and interrupting me for various reasons. I became impatient and yelled at them to get back in the house. I remember the looks on their faces. Who was this wicked witch yelling at them? Certainly it wasn't their Queen Mom. Oh yes, it was.

What made me yell that day when I hadn't before? I don't know. I do know that I valued getting the window trim painted more than taking care of my girls. Unfortunately, that wasn't the last time I lost my temper with them.

I'm not alone. This topic is so hot that Oprah Winfrey had Julie Ann Barnhill (international speaker and author of *She's Gonna Blow!*) on her show to discuss the issue of mommy anger. The original show ran October 2002 and aired at least two more times.

In the Presence of Anger

What is going on? We love our kids and hate to lose our tempers with them. But our lives are always changing. Many times we are caught off guard and don't know how to respond to the changes. Reality often shatters our expectations. What are we supposed to do now?

We get angry.

My recurring plea to God is, "Show me the right thing to do."

Dr. Gary Smalley, president and founder of Smalley Relationship Center, states, "Anger is a secondary emotion, not a primary feeling. It arises out of *fear, frustration, hurt* or some combination of the three."[1] I *fear* my kids won't obey, so I get angry. I *get frustrated* I won't accomplish my agenda, so I get angry. I am *hurt* because my teen chooses to be disobedient, even after my years of faithfully loving and disciplining. I get angry.

My recurring plea to God is, "Show me the right thing to do." If I know the right thing to do in a situation, I am more than halfway to having victory and relieving my suffering. Yet with changing life situations comes the uncertainty of how to respond or proceed. We don't have the information, insight, or perspective we need.

You are not a bad mom. Your kids are not bad kids. It's just that we all need some help to get going on the right track—and then some encouragement to stay on it.

 Frustration + wrong perspective = angry mom.

When you get angry, what do you fear? Why are you frustrated? Why are you hurt? Think over the most recent time you got angry. (OK, the most recent may be too tender. Think about a time last week.) Which of these emotions caused you to react in anger? On that chicken-pox-window-painting day, I was not afraid or hurt. I was frustrated because I had already been stuck at home for a week, caring for one sick child and one active preschool child. Now that Princess Two had the chicken pox, we would be stuck for another week. *Could I just get the window trim painted and have something to show for my time?* Frustration + wrong perspective = angry mom.

Nothing causes me more pain than to examine the mistakes I have made as a mom. But let's not beat ourselves up. God certainly won't. "If we [freely] admit that we have sinned and confess our sins, He is faithful and just (true to His own nature and promises) and will forgive our sins [dismiss our lawlessness] and [continuously] cleanse us from all unrighteousness [everything not in conformity to His will in purpose, thought, and action]" (1 John 1:9, *AMP*). You may need to reread that verse slowly, breathing in its healing truth. Give your past sins and failures to God. He took care of them through Jesus' blood. Because of the death of Jesus, anyone who has accepted him is now perfect in God's sight. We stand in the presence of God—holy, blameless, and without a single fault.

Causes of Anger

Knowing that God accepts you, ask him to show you what is causing your anger. Are you frustrated that your children aren't obeying you? Are you frustrated because you don't know how to get results with them? So are many, many parents. That's why that supernanny has her own TV program! Are you fearful that others will think you're not a good mom because your kids act out at the store? Do you fear your teen is lying to you? Are you hurt because your child doesn't seem to like you?

The answer may not have anything to do with your children at all. Are you frustrated carrying the whole burden of parenting because the children's father won't help (or because there *is* no father)? Are you frustrated that you can't find the time you want to give to your children because you must work to keep the bills paid? Are you tired, strapped financially, having relational problems with others, experiencing health problems, or too busy experiencing your own life?

Acknowledging the problem will help lift the load. Now talk to God about it and ask his wisdom. What can you do to make changes to improve your situation? If you can't change your situation, God knows that. Or he'll find a way you haven't thought of! He will be faithful to you and your kids when you are doing what he has shown you to do. Here is a verse to think on: "Those who honor me I will honor, but those who despise me will be disdained" (1 Samuel 2:30).

Once you have discovered the source (or sources) of your anger, refuse to sit and wallow in a puddle of self-pity. Move on to finding solutions to the things that cause you to lose it with your dear prince or princess.

You've Lost Your Authority

In *The Kingdom,* our fairy tale in chapter 1, the king and queen didn't know how to handle the prince and princess's disobedience, so they left the nanny in charge of discipline. When the decision was hers, she gave them what they wanted. By age thirteen the prince decided he would rule. The king and queen stood by helplessly.

Be aware that the way you were raised may or may not be God's plan for your kids. Even if you know you want to raise your children differently, realize you have tapes from the past playing in your head. Separate the truth in those tapes from the lies. Acknowledge that what you're doing isn't working and that you need to make some changes.

The how-tos for every area of discipline are too numerous to mention here, but we will continually discuss training and discipline throughout the book. The appendix at the end of this chapter (page 83) has age-appropriate guidelines for discipline from the Focus on Your Child Web site (a division of Focus on the Family). These guidelines will give you a great start in planning how to effectively discipline your little royals. This in turn will relieve your frustration level, thereby eliminating the anger.

 The way you were raised may or may not be God's plan for your kids.

New royal decrees should always be communicated to the children *before* they are implemented. For example, if you decide that when your five-year-old lies he must sit in the corner for five minutes, tell him. Then when he lies, act. Don't say, "Now, sweetie, remember what Mommy said about lying. Don't do it again, or I will have to put you in the corner." That only teaches him that he can continue to lie with no consequences and that you don't mean what you say. Instead, you might say (with your calm voice), "Alex, you lied to Mommy. Remember the consequence of lying—five minutes on a chair in the corner. I'll start the timer, and you can get down when it goes off." Now you have effectively disciplined Prince Alex in the area of lying . . . and without losing your temper.

My friend Angie has a discipline chart on her refrigerator. It lists the crime and the corresponding discipline. That way the king and queen are on the same page, and no one has to remember the rules. Consistency pays off.

You're Embarrassed by Your Kids' Behavior

Last weekend at Kelsey's band concert (like I said, it's the season that keeps on going), a family with two toddlers was sitting two rows in front of us. The younger child was about eighteen months old. She looked at us and laughed, so we smiled. Then she stuck out her tongue. What were we to do? More smiling only encouraged her, and looking away from that adorable face seemed mean. We didn't have to wonder for long. Her grandfather saw her and jumped up from his seat. He shot a look-to-kill our way, grabbed her arm, and seethed a threat under his breath. The toddler was upset for a few minutes; then she went back to her antics.

This man exhibited the-pot-is-about-to-boil-over anger. He reminded me of Jadis, the White Witch, in the movie *The*

Chronicles of Narnia: The Lion, the Witch and the Wardrobe. Jadis tried to convince naive Edmund that she was the Queen of Narnia by indulging him with Turkish delight and promising him the power to rule over his brother and sisters. Their conversation went well until Edmund ignorantly said something to anger her. She lashed out at him, quickly realized her mistake, and got back into Queen of Narnia character.

The White Witch was <u>not</u> the Queen of Narnia. She would always be a witch. But not us. We <u>are</u> the Queen Moms, even though we forget it sometimes.

Haven't we queens all done the reverse and slipped into our White Witch character while in public? When our kids are out of control in public, they know they can get away with more. And we seem to either let them . . . or blow up.

The White Witch was *not* the Queen of Narnia. She would always be a witch. But not us. We *are* the Queen Moms, even though we forget it sometimes.

The issue of the children's behavior in public has a two-part solution.

First, don't leave home without a plan. What will you do when the four-year-old prince starts throwing groceries out of the cart as fast as you put them in? If you have already formed a plan, you simply follow through. When the prince knows you mean what you say, he is less likely to misbehave in the store. Remember, consistency is key to a successful reign.

Secondly, realize that everyone's children disobey. No family is as perfect as it seems. I know it is hard to accept that other people are seeing your child's imperfections (or horrors—yours!), especially if the other family appears to have a spotless record. But we do not live to please others. We live to please God alone. When we care too deeply what others think, we are putting them on the throne that belongs to God. This is idolatry. For many years I have battled the dragon of caring what others think. The following verses have helped immensely:

- Fearing people is a dangerous trap, but to trust the LORD means safety (Proverbs 29:25, *NLT*).
- Obviously, I'm not trying to be a people pleaser! No, I am trying to please God. If I were still trying to please people, I would not be Christ's servant (Galatians 1:10, *NLT*).
- We are not trying to please men but God, who tests our hearts (1 Thessalonians 2:4).

Don't these verses lift a heavy burden? We don't have to please anyone but God. In fact, we are not to try to please anyone other than God. We are free to learn how to raise our children according to God's plan and do it without concern that other people won't approve.

You're Trying to Compete with Others

Sometimes unrealistic expectations—for ourselves and our kids—cause frustration, which leads to anger. In my twenty years of parenting, I finally learned that the fastest way to destroy my confident, Queen Mom attitude was to look at another family and play the comparison game. This leads to all kinds of misery. We feel as if we are making progress at this mom thing until a supermom enters the room. She makes the Proverbs 31 woman look like a wimp. This supermom is involved in PTA, rides in a car pool to work, teaches Sunday school, coaches softball, and runs errands to dozens of stores. She does all this and still looks great. How can I compete with that? I didn't even get my bed made before I left for Bible study this morning.

I am so proud of and pleased with our princesses (even though they are far from perfect) until I look at a supermom's kids. Just a glance over the proverbial fence, and I see that my kids aren't as accomplished on their musical instruments as the neighbor's kids. My girls don't excel in sports—they don't even play sports. They don't exhibit the boundless **talk-show**-host charisma and exuberance that the neighbors do. For a split second I yearn for my kids to know how to knit a sweater or run a mile in record time. My yearning quickly turns to despair—if I were a better mother, I would be teaching my kids origami on a rainy afternoon instead of letting them chill . . .

Good grief! Snap out of this, woman!

Quit comparing your kingdom to those around you. A family I know seems to be doing everything perfectly. Their kids excel in every way. I used to look at them and feel like such a failure. But God showed me that they are following his plan for *them.* That plan would be a disaster in my family. First, my husband would never agree; next, my kids would run screaming from our house. I have learned to be content doing what God has planned for us.

I must continually evaluate my decisions and goals to make sure they are in line with what God wants for me and my kids. What other families are doing is not related. Once I am in line with God's plan, I stress less. God's plan is tailor-made for us and our kids, and he doesn't demand more from us than we can do. There is no need to stress or become frustrated and angry when we let God order our agendas.

Knowing your child's limits (emotionally, physically, mentally) is important. The wise mom recognizes when her child has had enough. When Princess One was a baby, she had a small window of time in the morning when she was happy. She was content long enough for me to grocery shop, but by the time I was checking out, she was tired and hungry and coming unglued. I couldn't get upset; she was a baby. She knew she needed to eat and sleep, and I couldn't expect her to do otherwise.

There is no need to stress or become frustrated and angry when we let God order our agendas.

Young children (and some adults I know) are overwhelmed when they are told to pick up the toys. All they see is a huge mess, and they have no idea how to begin. Princess Three was often sent to clean up her room. Each time I checked on her progress, little had changed. Was this disobedience, or was she overwhelmed with what I asked her to do? The frustration on her face was so pathetic, I knew she was overwhelmed. So I figured out a way to help her. I bought storage bins to keep her toys sorted. Then I gave her only the amount of direction she could handle: "Kerry, put away all the stuffed animals." After that task was completed, I said, "Kerry, put away the doll clothes." And so we continued until the room was clean. Sure, it took more of my time, but she learned to organize and clean her room. Princess Three was all smiles because she'd discovered how to reign in her little kingdom.

Children have emotional limits. My three-year-old nephew had enough of being with family one Easter. He hunted Easter eggs before breakfast, went to church, came to Aunt Brenda's for a nice lunch, and hunted more eggs with his twin sister and twelve cousins. He was tired of everyone (and so was Aunt Brenda!). He was in his mom's arms when someone came up and tried to engage him in play. But he'd had enough. He had nothing left for play, so he grunted and turned his head into his mother's bosom. The wise Queen Mom knows when her child is spent, and she will not demand more.

Examine your expectations and see how realistic and important they are. Where did your agenda come from? Is it helpful, or does it add stress to your life? After my chicken-pox girls ran outside for the second time, I should have realized it was not a good day to paint windows. I should have put the mess away, gone inside, and played with them. The windows were *my* agenda, not God's. Trying to paint the windows that day did not help anyone; it only added stress.

"There is a time for everything, and a season for every activity under heaven" (Ecclesiastes 3:1). These famous words are vital for Queen Mom's survival. We cannot do everything now. We need to ask God what is important for now, what can wait, and what's not important at all. He is faithful and he will tell us.

The wise Queen Mom knows when her child is spent, and she will not demand more.

If you need wisdom—if you want to know what God wants you to do—ask him, and he will gladly tell you. He will not resent your asking. But when you ask him, be sure that you really expect him to answer, for a doubtful mind is as unsettled as a wave of the sea that is driven and tossed by the wind. People like that should not expect to receive anything from the Lord. They can't make up their minds. They waver back and forth in everything they do (James 1:5-8, *NLT*).

Be ready to hear God and make changes. And one more thing: look at Jesus. He didn't do everything when he was on earth. He focused on his mission from God, preaching the good news.

You're Tired Physically, Emotionally, and Spiritually

We need to examine the many factors that influence the way we relate to our kids—to see what may be causing us to . . . well, lose it.

> I remembered Psalm 123:1: "I lift up my eyes to you, to you whose throne is in heaven." I could rest because God had everything under control.

Let's start with physical factors. Nothing makes me crankier than not getting my required sleep. Recently I went through an extremely stressful situation that caused me not to sleep well. The stress, combined with the fatigue, contributed to my being edgy and crabby. Finally I realized I couldn't go on worrying and not sleeping. I prayed for God to give me his perspective and his peace for this situation. He did, but I had to continually let go of my worries and receive the truth he presented. (Why do we find it so comforting to hold on to our troubles? It's like using a cactus as a security blanket.) One night, as I lay my head on the pillow, God reminded me, *I'm on my throne.* Then I remembered

Psalm 123:1: "I lift up my eyes to you, to you whose throne is in heaven." I could rest because God had everything under control.

My type A personality drives me to want to get a lot accomplished in a day. God has reminded me of a few key truths:

- 👑 No matter how much I get done, there is always more to do.
- 👑 If I don't get a job done today, it will still be there tomorrow.
- 👑 I need to discern what is important, urgent, and not necessary. The not necessary has to go; the urgent has to be done, but not rule; and the important cannot be put off.

These truths help me keep a proper perspective and honor my priorities. Jesus is our example of how to manage life. He had balance in his life—so should we.

Other physical conditions may contribute to your fatigue. I have blood sugar issues. When I feel my blood sugar dropping, I experience edginess, loss of concentration, headache, and dizziness. I know I need to eat healthy food every couple of hours to maintain my blood sugar and feel good. (It's hard to keep a royal figure when I'm on a two-hour feeding schedule!) Hormonal issues, such as premenstrual syndrome and perimenopause, can cause mood swings. Don't rule out depression. It creeps up, and you may not be aware of the gradual changes in your personality. If you are unable to control your crabbiness with healthy lifestyle changes, please get a complete physical from a health-care provider. Taking care of yourself is one of the best things you can do for your family.

God created us to be social creatures, some of us more than others. My husband, Gene, can go months without a heart-to-heart talk with anyone other than me. I start to shrivel up and die if I go more than two weeks without serious communication with my friends. Don't isolate yourself. We moms need to see that we aren't the only ones struggling. We have a lot to offer each other.

We shouldn't underestimate the importance of our spiritual health.

The girls in the young moms group at my church are passionate about seeing each other. They help each other emotionally. They have each other over with their assorted children in tow. The meal is simple—apples, cheese, and crackers. They've decided not to worry that their houses aren't in perfect order for those visits.

We shouldn't underestimate the importance of our spiritual health. My princesses have always been high-maintenance girls. They got up early and didn't nap long. When they were up, they played actively and talked to me a lot. They have turned into bright, young women who communicate well with peers and adults. But with all the time I spent interacting with them, I often didn't make time for building my relationship with the Lord.

One day I was expressing my frustration about the anger issue to an older, mature, godly woman. Her reply was sweet but to the point, "Brenda, how is your quiet time with the Lord?" *Uh, well, what quiet time?* In that moment, God made an appointment with me. He put on my heart to meet with him at 5:30 AM every day. The next weekend I bought my own alarm clock, and I have consistently (not perfectly, but in the 90 percent range) met with

God at that time every morning. The difference in my life is huge. I can't imagine what kind of wife and mom I would be today if I had not accepted this invitation from God.

Now breathe, moms. I'm not talking in-depth, monklike study and solitude. Start small—ten or fifteen minutes alone in God's presence. Pray and listen to God. Get a devotional book to direct your thoughts to God. When the princesses were small, I used my time in the shower to talk to God. Now I have more time and energy to meet with him. I have several books I like to use as devotionals—something to springboard me to better focus on God. (My personal favorites are: *Let Go* by Fenelon, *My Utmost for His Highest* by Oswald Chambers, and *Secrets of the Vine* by Bruce Wilkinson.)

· ·

Anger is a fact of life. But when we acknowledge it and ask the King of kings for help, he can transform a Queen Mom's iron fist into a gentle, leading hand.

Royal Decree

I know this anger issue is a tender wound in our hearts. We love our kids fiercely. We don't want to lose our tempers. We are embarrassed and ashamed when we do. Admit this area of sin to your heavenly Father. Now use this information, getting more help if needed, and move forward to enjoy your princes and princesses.

Royal Inquiry

1. What is usually the primary feeling behind your anger—fear, frustration, or hurt? Is it a combination?

2. Are you more likely to feel you've lost your authority, be embarrassed by your kids' behavior, or compare your family to other families? What did you learn that will help you?

3. Do you frequently feel physically or emotionally exhausted? If yes, do you see a connection to how you handle your anger? What will you do to address this issue and gain victory over your anger?

4. Have you neglected your spiritual health? Write down three small steps you can take to turn this situation around.

Appendix

Following is a great guideline for disciplining kids. Understanding the points presented can help you respond to your children with love, rather than responding with anger.

What to Expect from Your Child

Age-Appropriate Discipline

All parents seek disciplinary techniques that work. However, not all techniques work for all ages or for all children. Use this list as a guide for age-appropriate discipline.

Distraction. Infants (birth to 18 months) typically do not need strong disciplinary measures. When babies "misbehave" they are often exploring and testing their boundaries. Simply directing a baby's attention elsewhere may solve the problem.

Time-Out. Many parents use time-out for all behaviors all the time. However, for time-out to work, it should be used as one tool in an arsenal of other discipline techniques for ages 2 to 8. Some basic guidelines for time-out include:

- Make it short—1 minute for each year of your child's age.
- Eliminate reinforcers. Your child should not be able to play, watch television, etc.
- Use a timer. Restart the time if your child leaves time-out.
- Use other discipline techniques if time-out does not work.

Removal of privileges. Taking away toys, activities or outings can be an effective way to manage inappropriate behavior for children ages 18 months and older. To make sure this technique works for you:

- 👑 Choose a meaningful privilege that your child will greatly miss.
- 👑 Follow through on warnings to remove privileges.
- 👑 Remove the item for a short amount of time (differs by age—several hours for a 2-year-old but several days for a 12-year-old).

Natural consequences. Parents do not need to get involved in order for natural consequences to take effect. For example, if your child refuses to eat dinner, instead of developing a power struggle, allow her to go to bed without eating. She will naturally be hungry in the morning and will be certain to eat. (Appropriate for children 2 and older.)

Logical consequences. This is a punishment that fits the crime. Suppose your child throws a ball in the house and breaks a vase. She could be asked to work off the value of the vase or use her allowance to buy a new one.

Spanking. Spanking typically works best with ages 2 to 6. It should be used only for specific, purposeful misbehavior and should never be done in anger. As with other techniques, spanking should be used as one of many discipline tools.

· ·

chapter five

The Prince and Princess Throw a Royal Temper Tantrum

Helping Kids Handle Their Emotions

Of course, the king and queen put a stop to whatever plan was in the works. This led to temper tantrums by the little royals.

This was not the first temper tantrum for the prince and princess. Early on they'd learned this technique, and it had served them well. Too bad the king and queen didn't take time to help their children deal with their emerging emotions.

Our princes and princesses live for themselves. They will get angry when they don't get what they want or don't understand why life isn't going their way. It is our job to help them understand all this. If we don't, the world will eventually supply *its* answers.

This chapter is a hard one for me. Why? As a member of the Good Moms Club (you are one too, or else you wouldn't be reading this book), I care so deeply about my kids' emotional health, I often take on the dreaded "mommy guilt." This causes me to feel that if my kids aren't doing well, I am responsible. It's a commonly believed myth. Actually it is a lie. Let me state this lie succinctly: *If my child is doing poorly in any area, I must be a bad mom.* I allowed Satan to beat me with this club for far too long. Don't let him do it to you.

> I care so deeply about my kids' emotional health, I often take on the dreaded "mommy guilt."

God's Part, Our Part

I am responsible for trying to be the best mom I can be, using every resource God has given me. These resources include his wisdom, the guidance of the Holy Spirit, instruction from the Bible, godly counsel—written and spoken, and professional counsel if the circumstance demands it. When I seek God's wisdom, he is responsible for the results in my kids.

Hear this important concept clearly. It is *not* a ticket to give up on your kids when they are not responding to your parenting. No, this is a call to never stop trying to discover how best to relate to your child. But after we have done all God has shown us, the results are up to him. Living with this understanding releases you from guilt and a sense of failure when your child doesn't respond as you hoped he would.

Ephesians 6:13 has been my sustenance through some shaky parenting experiences. I like the way the *Amplified Bible* explains what we are to do: "Put on God's complete armor, that you may be able to resist and stand your ground on the evil day [of danger], and, having done all [the crisis demands], to stand [firmly in your place]." After we have done everything we are responsible to do, we are to stand firm in the Lord—not to worry, not to get angry or frustrated, but to stand firm and confident that our Lord is working on behalf of us and our kids.

Paul assures us,

> No, despite all these things, overwhelming victory is ours through Christ, who loved us. And I am convinced that nothing can ever separate us from his love. Death can't, and life can't. The angels can't, and the demons can't. Our fears for today, our worries about tomorrow, and even the powers of hell can't keep God's love away. Whether we are high above the sky or in the deepest ocean, nothing in all creation will ever be able to separate us from the love of God that is revealed in Christ Jesus our Lord (Romans 8:37-39, *NLT*).

Our families are in God's hands!

God Helps Us Discover the Source

Are you ready to move on to helping your kids with their emotions? Just like us, our kids have reasons for getting angry. They don't wake up in the morning and say, "I'm going through the whole day mad at everyone." (I know it seems like some kids do.) Our job is to discover the reason for their anger and help them deal with it. A quick review of chapter 4 reminds us that anger is a response to fear, frustration, or hurt. A child may be frustrated because he is not getting his way, so he gets angry. He may be fearful that you aren't hearing him, and that causes him to be angry.

 "No, despite all these things, overwhelming victory is ours through Christ, who loved us."

Dr. Gary Smalley states that everyone has a core fear—a fear that is at the center of who we are. Here is his list of common core fears:

1. Helpless, powerless, impotent, or controlled
2. Rejected, as if people are closing me out of their lives
3. Abandoned or left behind, as in divorce
4. Disconnected from others or alone
5. Feel like a failure
6. Unloved, as if no one could love me
7. Defective, as if something is wrong with me, as if I'm the problem
8. Inadequate, as if I just don't measure up to others like I should[1]

Just reading the list pierces my heart. I hate to think that my princesses have these feelings, because I know that these statements are not true of them. These statements reflect how we allow others to make us feel. They are not really who we are as God's followers. Here *is* the truth:

1. I am not powerless. I have power from God (Ephesians 1:19, 20).
2. I am not rejected. I am accepted by God (Colossians 1:21, 22).
3. I am not abandoned. God has told me, "I will never fail you. I will never forsake you" (Hebrews 13:5, *NLT*).
4. I am not alone. God is "an ever-present help" (Psalm 46:1).
5. I am not a failure. I may fail at times, but that is not who I am. I am a new creation in Christ (Colossians 2:10; 2 Corinthians 5:17, 18).

6. I am not unloved. God loves me deeply and passionately (1 John 4:9, 10).
7. I am not defective. God "created my inmost being." I am "wonderfully made" (Psalm 139:13, 14).
8. I am not inadequate. I have the Lord, so "I have everything I need" (Psalm 23:1, *NLT*). And "I can do everything" I need to do, with his help (Philippians 4:13, *NLT*).

I know that the core fears listed above are not true about me; nevertheless, I have felt each one. Let's take the feeling we have right now—the desire to help our children see past the lies of their fears—and use it to motivate us in helping our kids with their anger. When our kids are angry, they are hurting. They need our help, not our anger or judgment. This is difficult to keep in mind because most of the time they misbehave in response to their anger, and we must deal with both the misbehavior and the anger.

God Helps Us Discern the Expressions

Children develop different ways of expressing their emotions. Children fall into two categories—the verbally and physically expressive, and the nonexpressive. If you have more than one child, you've probably figured this out. Come to think of it, most of the adults I know handle their emotions the same way.

 When our kids are angry, they are hurting. They need our help, not our anger or judgment.

We usually think of the outward expression of anger when we think of inappropriate anger. When I was a child in the '60s, the choices on TV were limited. My sisters and I always looked forward to the once-a-year special programs. One special that we loved was Rodgers & Hammerstein's *Cinderella*. In this 1957 version of the old tale, Cinderella represents innocence and goodness, her fairy godmother represents hope and help for those who can't help themselves, and the wicked stepsisters represent evil.

Why did those two become so evil? Because their mother, the wicked stepmother, indulged them and never disciplined them. So when they got angry they exploded—most often on poor Cindy. Just think how the story might have turned out if the stepsisters had had a mom who cared enough to help them handle their anger.

The boundaries of the outward expression of anger are limitless; we couldn't even imagine them all. We will discuss the more common outward expressions of anger.

My friend Linda wondered how to deal with her toddler's outburst. Princess Amy was mad, so she angrily pushed some papers off the coffee table—papers Linda was working on. It's vital to know why Amy was mad. Was she feeling helpless because she couldn't get her way with the queen? Was she feeling abandoned or disconnected because the queen had been on the phone too long and was ignoring her? Did she feel like a failure because she couldn't get a toy to work? Or was she feeling unloved because of the arrival of her baby sister?

If Princess Amy was mad because she couldn't get her way, she needed to be disciplined for disobedience. If she was angry because Linda was chatting on the phone too long, then Linda should get off the phone immediately and stop Amy from making a mess. Linda should tell Amy this behavior is not acceptable and then give her some positive attention.

Remember, we need to have realistic expectations for our kids. We can't expect a toddler to behave perfectly while we linger on the phone and ignore her. The same goes for the frustration about getting a toy to work; take time to help the child with the toy and teach her not to be destructive.

Passive-aggressive behavior drives me nuts because I don't know what the child is thinking.

One of our princesses expresses her anger verbally, and while I hated the outbursts, I was thankful because I always knew what she was feeling. The other two princesses don't explode in their anger but let it seep out. This is called passive-aggressive behavior. *Merriam-Webster's Medical Dictionary* defines passive-aggressive as "being, marked by, or displaying behavior characterized by expression of negative feelings, resentment, and aggression in an unassertive way (as through procrastination, stubbornness, and unwillingness to communicate)."[2] You may have noticed that in marriage, passive-aggressive behavior is often displayed when a husband asks his wife, "What's wrong?" and she answers, "Nothing."

Passive-aggressive behavior drives me nuts because I don't know what the child is thinking, so I assume the worst. This morning I was sucked in again. Princess Three asked for apple butter on her toast. Princess Three is at that dreaded age of hormonal ups and downs. One minute she is her sweet, carefree self; then without warning her feelings become fragile. When I told her we were out of apple butter, the expression on her face looked as it might if I had just told a five-year-old there is no Santa Claus. I offered jelly. No help. I asked if she was OK. No change. Then her been-there-done-that teen sister entered the room and said, "Mom, she's fine."

A smile broke out. She *was* fine. She was teasing me—and she sure knew how to do it! It was a joke. We all had a good laugh, and no harm was done.

However, we need to recognize when our kids are using P/A behavior as a habitual response to discipline or chores or anything else that they don't like. This technique is especially effective when paired with a shy personality. I have learned that many shy kids are not the delicate flowers they portray themselves to be. They are stubborn and tough and will persevere to get their way.

My friend Sara has several children. She realized early on that when there was a fight between the children, she would never know the truth because each child told only his side. Now, to resolve conflicts, Sara has the involved parties sit on the sofa and work out the argument themselves. Sara is close by so she can keep things fair. This approach works well on all the children but one. This child is her "shy and quiet" one. When he is doing time on the sofa, he never gives in or makes any concessions. He never admits any wrong. Do you see the anger this child is silently screaming? No door slamming. No insults. No loud outbursts. Just stubbornness until he achieves victory.

 Anger is an emotion given to us by God to tell us that something in our lives needs attention.

Dennis and Barbara Rainey give some sobering advice in their book *Parenting Today's Adolescent*: "Passive anger is deceptive, because it seems easier to tolerate than the behavior of a child who screams and throws a fit. But it's a pay-now-or-pay-later proposition. All anger that is not identified and addressed will bear bitter fruit later in obstinate attitudes, irrational behavior to punish parents or other authority figures, physical symptoms, or depression."[3] Just because one of our children is not verbally screaming for attention doesn't mean he doesn't need it and desperately want it.

Proper Preparation Before Action

Goal: a conversation with your child, during which you can help him discover and verbalize what is bothering him and then help him come up with an appropriate response for his anger. How to have such a conversation?

Well, a good queen gets herself together before she can reign successfully. Check at the door your emotions, attitudes, and laundry list of the issues you have with your child. You need to be cool and compassionate—a good listener without an agenda. Remember how patient God is with you. One more area of preparation is needed before anger management can be implemented with your child: if your child is the type who outwardly expresses his anger, find a time to talk with him when he is not stressed or angry.

A Plan of Action

Here's a run-through of your plan:

During the conversation, ask your child how he feels about the way he acts when he gets angry. He may become defensive about his actions, but assure him you are there to help, not criticize. Reassure him that anger is an emotion given to us by God to tell us that something in our lives needs attention.

Explore what makes your child mad (remember Dr. Smalley's list of core fears). Explore how he feels. Ask him for ideas concerning how he could express his anger appropriately without hurting anything or anyone (physically or emotionally). Be ready with suggestions if he is clueless. I have done this with a princess, and it is helpful. She does not like expressing herself angrily. Talking with her brings out her true feelings. That is key to getting resolution to the source of her anger.

Communication is key to helping all types of children properly respond to their feelings.

This talk will not be a once-and-for-all fix-it but will be necessary from time to time as your child grows and changes. Several months ago, I had another of these talks with one princess. I asked why, a few days previously, she had responded in her anger with a mean comment to me. She said, "Because I knew it would hurt you. I didn't mean it." *Well, I'm so glad we cleared the air!* Of course it hurt, but now I know the truth—this is how she lashes out in anger; and truly, under the anger, she loves me.

What needed to be communicated to this princess was that she is free to express that she is angry with me, but she must not attack me personally. She still doesn't agree with all my royal rulings, but she has learned to express herself without attacking the queen.

You will remind your child that all actions have consequences. So when he sins in his anger (i.e., hits his sister or puts his foot through the wall), he will need to suffer the consequences for those inappropriate expressions of anger.

Our kids learn more from our actions than our words. I know, I hate that too. Stay with me here—don't let a load of guilt take you down now. Remember in chapter 4 how we confessed our parenting failures to God and were made clean? Hopefully, you are making a plan of how you will appropriately handle your anger in the future. If you haven't been a good example in this area, admit it to your child—he already knows it. Tell him you have confessed to God and that together both of you will learn to express and deal with anger appropriately. Help him determine his personal plan.

After your conversation . . . the next time your prince is angry, watch to see how he reacts. Is he following his plan? It may take just a knowing look from you to remind him. After he cools down, you may talk to him about the issue.

Now you're ready to actually put your plan into action. You need to communicate well, share biblical truth, and discipline if necessary.

Communicate Well

Communication is key to helping all types of children properly respond to their feelings. For years Dr. James Dobson has advised parents to try to get behind the eyes of their kids to see how they perceive a situation and then relate to them from that perspective.

This is where the relationship you've been building with your child comes in. Know your child. Would he prefer to talk at bedtime? right when he gets home from school? while the two of you do something together (bake, fold clothes, watch TV)? only when it can be in his room with no siblings nearby?

Pick the right time and place; then gently ask leading questions. Use Dr. Smalley's list of core fears as a guide. Your prince may not know what is bothering him, so this might be an expedition for both of you. Then listen. Even when you *know* the answer to his situation, keep your lips together and listen. You're building relationship here as well as helping him with his issue.

When he has finished expressing himself, if he hasn't discovered the cause of his anger, ask leading questions to help him do so. Then show him the truth of the situation. Yes, life is not fair. Yes, you know he is hurt. Explain to him how Jesus suffered for him. That wasn't fair either. People were mean to Jesus. He knows hurt. He feels your child's hurt.

The mere fact that you are making the effort to communicate with and help your child will not be lost on him. Sensing your love and concern, he will be more open to future similar conversations.

Share Biblical Truth

Use God's Word to show your child the right thing to do. In their book *Parents' Guide to the Spiritual Mentoring of Teens,* Joe White and Jim Weidmann explain the importance of getting your kids in the Word:

> The second basic element of the faith we aim to instill in our teens is a head filled with applied wisdom from Scripture. After all, the Bible is God's personally given love letter to mankind, the primary means by which He reveals to us His character and His will. The Bible says of itself in 2 Timothy 3:16-17, 'All Scripture is God-breathed and is useful for teaching, rebuking, correcting and training in righteousness, so that the man [or woman] of God may be thoroughly equipped for every good work.' Thus, if our kids are to grow in their relationship with Him, they need to study it, learn it, and know how to apply its truths to life's challenges and choices.[4]

You can openly and effectively share God's Word with your

kids. You don't have to be a Bible scholar. I'm not. But I have discovered three tools that help me take "the sword of the Spirit, which is the word of God" (Ephesians 6:17) and use it:

The first tool is the concordance in the back of my Bible. A concordance lists key the words in the Bible and the verses in which they are used. So if, for example, one of my girls is having trouble with friends gossiping or she was caught gossiping, I would look up the word *gossip* and find several verses that discuss the ugly truth of gossiping. I would read these with my daughter and let the power of God's Word speak to her heart. The appendices in the back of many Bibles list verses for different situations or topics.

The next tool is similar, but oh, so twenty-first century. The Web site www.BibleGateway.com has a comprehensive concordance with every word in the Bible and every time it is used. You can also look up Scriptures topically, do a word search, or look for a specific verse. The site has many different translations and a commentary. It is hundreds of dollars' worth of Bible reference books on one Web site. (There are other similar sites.)

The last tool consists of the notes I take when I hear a sermon or Bible lesson. Sometimes I write in my Bible, sometimes in my journal. I make my own index in the back of my Bible with verses that interest me. In the back of other books I read, I also index topics that interest me. This system helps me find quickly what I need on a given topic.

God's Word works powerfully in the hearts of kids. Let's not deprive them of its power because we fear we aren't qualified to share it or we fear they may not receive it well. Both fears are based on Satan's lies. God doesn't want us to live in fear. Look back at Dr. Smalley's list. How many of these issues could be avoided if we believed deep in our hearts how much God loves and accepts us?

> God's Word works powerfully in the hearts of kids. Let's not deprive them of its power because we fear we aren't qualified to share it or we fear they may not receive it well.

I challenge you to put the following verse in your heart; then help your princes and princesses put it in their hearts: "The LORD your God has arrived to live among you. He is a mighty savior. He will rejoice over you with great gladness. With his love, he will calm all your fears. He will exult over you by singing a happy song" (Zephaniah 3:17, *NLT*). Imagine the work the Holy Spirit could do in your child's upset heart when the two of you say this verse together! The truth in this verse encompasses every core fear.

Discipline If Necessary

If, after all great communication efforts and sharing the Word, your little prince is still unrepentant, he is asking for discipline. Give him discipline that will get his attention. Discipline needs to cause affliction to get his attention. This will look different for each child, depending on his or her temperament and age. Discover what works best for your child, and then be consistent.

If your kids don't seem to respond to anything, the following books are insightful for dealing with the more challenging personalities: *You Can't Make Me (But I Can Be Persuaded)* by Cynthia Tobias and *Aaron's Way: The Journey of a Strong-Willed Child* by Kendra Smiley.

Seek Professional Help

When you have done everything you can but your child is not making progress, you may need to consider Christian counseling. Your child may need someone to release his emotions with. Talk with your pastor or youth pastor. He may counsel with your child or be able to recommend a counselor.

Recently a friend, her husband, and their teenage son went for a first appointment with a Christian counselor and talked at length. Even the next day the atmosphere in the home was better. It will take more meetings with the counselor to work through the issues, but this teen's emotional valve was released by having a qualified counselor to hear him, understand him, and offer professional advice.

Your child may have a physical problem that is related to emotional issues and needs medical attention. Call your physician and explain the situation. Then let your child know he is going in for a physical; this is the truth. The doctor can look for and test for anything that might be causing an emotional imbalance.

• •

This is hard stuff, isn't it? Dealing with our kids' emotions is . . . well, emotional! The Lord will get us through, if we enlist and rely on his help.

Royal Decree

Here's another verse I encourage you to memorize. It will boost your confidence as you help your kids handle their emotions: "Now glory be to God! By his mighty power at work within us, he is able to accomplish infinitely more than we would ever dare to ask or hope" (Ephesians 3:20, *NLT*).

Royal Inquiry

1. Have you believed the lie "If my child is doing poorly in any area, I must be a bad mom"? If yes, throw off the lie and the guilt. Just determine to do everything you can to be the mom God designed you to be—not perfect, but the perfect mom for your child.

2. Look at **Dr. Smalley's** list of core fears on page 90. Identify how you respond to them. Identify how you perceive each of your children responding to them. This may take some time. It doesn't need to be done in one sitting.

3. Do you handle your anger outwardly or passive-aggressively? What about each of your children? Analyzing this is part of the process of getting to know them, relating to them, and disciplining them more effectively.

4. Are you reluctant to use the Bible in your parenting? Start by applying God's Word to your own core fears. Use the tools I mentioned to find help and encouragement for your core fears. If you need extra help, ask someone who is more experienced in the Word.

chapter six

Kingdom Boundaries Beat a Dictatorship Any Day

Setting Boundaries vs. Control

They stopped cold in their tracks when they saw what was taking place.

The prince and princess were sitting on the thrones. This time they weren't pretending to be the king and queen; they were running the court. They were giving orders to the cook, the gardener, the chambermaids, the knights, and anyone else they could find. The court was in chaos.

The king and queen approached their thrones. "Children, you need to step down and let us rule the kingdom."

The prince and princess acknowledged their parents with looks that said "Make us."

Aaarrrggghhh!! I want to scream when I see moms let their kids do whatever they want simply because the moms are too lazy or scared to set a boundary and enforce it. Who is on the throne here?

Princess One was the child who caused us to make a rule for everything. We made the rule, and she would abide by it to the letter—but not the intent. She often found a detour around the rule in order to get her way. So we disciplined her for disobeying what she knew we meant.

> **Boundaries are what our kids are screaming for when we don't step up and be the Queen Mom.**

For example, during her sophomore year, we allowed her to have instant messaging. She could talk on IM for twenty minutes per day. How could she find a loophole in that? At midnight she slipped onto IM and talked to a boy we never would have allowed her to hang out with. She rationalized that we hadn't specified *when* she was to use her minutes or *to whom* she could talk. Incidents like this resulted in grounding for three consecutive months. There were three such groundings for boundary challenges that year. Princess One thought she would never get out of the house!

And then we would make yet another rule.

On and on this process went. We made rules for everything—activities, music, clothes, quality of chores, computer . . . You name it, she challenged it. She marches to the beat of a different drummer. (So does her mother, but we have *different* different drummers.) Our goal was to give her room to be herself while we trained her to be responsible, kind, thoughtful, well mannered, and mature. Well, at least we were *trying*!

The Need for Boundaries

If I had to summarize this book in one word, that word would be *boundaries*. Boundaries are what our kids are screaming for when we don't step up and be the Queen Mom. When we are not providing a secure environment—one in which kids know their parents are in charge, what they can and can't do, and what the consequences for disobedience are—they act out in numerous ways:

- They challenge us
- They scream throughout grocery shopping trips.
- They hit their siblings.
- They sass us.
- They turn on an inappropriate TV show.
- They attach themselves to friends who aren't good for them.
- They do things to harm themselves.

Some kids who do these things have parents who *have* set boundaries in place. But more often, kids behave in these ways because they are crying out for our time and attention. They need for us to be in charge.

Recently at the grocery store, the clerk and I were discussing the joys of having daughters. The clerk took a quick U-turn from expressing her joy as she described her five-year-old's frequent sassing. This child's language was so disrespectful and rude that I was shocked and mind-boggled. It was clear to me that this child, by her actions, was screaming to her mom, "Who's in charge? If you won't take charge, I will."

Letting our kids live by their own rules is cruel. The real world certainly won't let them live by their own rules. Our jails are full of people who have tried. Bankruptcy and divorce courts are overrun with adults who tried to live by their own rules. (I know not everyone who has filed for bankruptcy or is divorced is at fault.) Our job is to raise our kids to be responsible, mature adults. This cannot happen without realistic boundaries.

In the movie *The Prince & Me*, the Danish prince decides to live by his own rules, outside the boundaries of his country. His father, the king, desperately wants him to be about the family business. The prince wants no part of this life, so he grabs some royal cash and his trusty butler and heads for America. It doesn't take long for him to party away his wealth, and he finds himself working as a busboy and living with a less-than-desirable roommate. The prince's reckless lifestyle caused his father to worry himself into an illness that quickly took his life. Funny. Life outside the boundaries had looked very exciting to the prince. It was a different story when he actually *was* outside the boundaries.

 Our job is to raise our kids to be responsible, mature adults. This cannot happen without realistic boundaries.

I am defining *boundary* as a limit or border put in place by the king and queen. Its purpose is to build the character of the young royal and keep him from physical, emotional, and spiritual harm. The boundaries should be as large as possible for the given situation and child, in order to give the child room to learn and to be the person God created him to be. Later in the chapter we will discuss the boundaries kids themselves need to set up for their own well-being.

Boundaries grow with the child. An infant has tight boundaries. It is highly important for Queen Mom to establish her reign with this new royal by getting him on *her* schedule and not the other way around. When he becomes a few months old, he can safely play within the boundaries of his playpen. As he grows to toddlerhood, he is out of the playpen and off and running, exploring his world and learning what is off limits (things like touching the stereo, computer, and stove). He still eats, naps, and goes to bed when his mom says it's time; but he is learning, exploring his interests, and becoming his own person.

I am defining <u>boundary</u> as a limit or border put in place by the king and queen. Its purpose is to build the character of the young royal and keep him from physical, emotional, and spiritual harm.

Our girls are each distinctive. They have the same mother and father, but they have different personalities, talents, likes, and dislikes. Gene and I set the boundaries for each daughter far enough out to give them room to grow. God has a great plan for each of them, and I want them to discover his plan and boldly and faithfully live it.

This past Christmas I gave the girls a gift that actually spelled out that truth to them. I found Christmas ornaments that read "Believe" and "Dream." They were die-cut metal and painted white with snowflake-like glitter. A letter from the king and me accompanied the ornaments. It read in part, "Believe in God, but not only *in* God; believe God. . . . Dream the dream God puts in your heart to be the person he made you to be and to live the vision he will give you." I want my girls to bloom into the special women God had in mind when he created them, and I want them to love him and know him. That can't happen if we don't give them room to be exactly as God designed them to be.

It also can't happen if we don't raise them with boundaries that will develop character, train and discipline them, and teach them to respect themselves and others. Boundaries are God's idea. He gave the first man and woman boundaries in the Garden of Eden when he told them not to "eat from the tree of the knowledge of good and evil." He had good reason. "For when you eat of it you will surely die" (Genesis 2:17). God had given them all of paradise to explore and enjoy, but this one tree was not to be touched—and that rule was for their good.

The Bible is full of boundaries for us, his children. He has a plan for us to live so we will glorify him; live in his peace and at peace with others; live lives that are satisfying because we are in his will; and be spared the heartache, pain, and consequences of living apart from God.

He gave us boundaries for our good.

Inappropriate Motives

Before we can get serious about setting and enforcing boundaries, we need to examine what motives might be roadblocks in this process. A key to being successful mothers is knowing what drives us. How can I make good decisions, be patient, not take things personally, and keep my perspective if my inner queen is a royal mess?

What are the motives that drive decisions concerning our kids? Let's look at three negative attitudes that might be influencing us.

How can I make good decisions, be patient, not take things personally, and keep my perspective if my inner queen is a royal mess?

Unwillingness to Let Go

When a mom doesn't want to let go of her growing child, each stage of development puts a pain in her heart. She may want to hold her infant through his nap because she loves the cuddling. She may be hesitant to let her child play at the home of a trusted friend because she can't stand to be separated from him. When the child starts school, this mom volunteers for everything so she can be near him.

Even when the child goes away to college, this mom is overly involved, calling often, not letting him deal with the realities of life. Pop culture has given such a mom the trademark name Helicopter Mom. ABC ran a news story on this parenting mutation: "Dr. Helen Johnson, a consultant on parental relations in higher education for some of America's top universities, says parents like Robyn are far too involved in their children's lives. 'The problem is, they're doing exactly what's wrong for their son or daughter. She's also crippling them in the sense that they are not going to understand that they can manage their own lives.'"[1]

Letting go can be especially hard on a mom with her last child. Just recently this hit me with Princess Three, Kerry. She has always been my cuddle bunny. The other day I tried to give her a peck on the cheek and a quick hug, and I didn't get my usual warm response.

I asked her, "Are you getting ready for Mom not to hug you so much?"

"Yeah."

That was it. Straightforward, with no emotion. Time to release her a bit more.

We will talk more about releasing in chapter 10.

Unwillingness to Follow Through

When a mom isn't sure of the appropriate boundary or how to enforce it, she may back off too far. Some kids are natural boundary pushers. They daily challenge our decisions. These kids can wreak havoc on a mom's confidence. Are we making the right decision? Are we too strict? None of the other moms have our rules . . . This is a hard place to be. I have been there. I want to help you confidently make your plan for parenting.

If you are married, enlist the help of your husband, especially when the little royals get to the I-know-everything-about-everything-and-you-know-nothing stage. (This can hit earlier than age twelve and may last through the late teens.) Men have a way of cutting through the emotions and confidently making and enforcing a decision.

If you are a single mom, I would still recommend getting the help of a trusted, positive man. I know, I know—one more thing to do. But this is important, especially if you have boys. God knows kids need both a mom and dad, so if there is no dad in the picture, ask God to show you a replacement. Pray for the right guy. Use the discernment God gave you, and solicit wise Christian counsel to make this decision. Know that God is working the other side of this situation too. When you find the right guy for the job, God will have been stirring him and guiding him to this exciting opportunity.

Sometimes moms don't want to hassle with enforcing the boundaries. This was the case for the king and queen in our fairy tale, *The Kingdom*. They knew there was a problem, but they didn't want to give the time and energy to fix it. They didn't want the prince and princess to become angry. They didn't want to seem mean, and they definitely did not want to change their plans to enforce discipline. So the boundaries were left wide open with no consequences.

Unwillingness to Confront

Let's say mom's personality is passive. She doesn't like conflict. She doesn't feel equipped to deal with this child. This is a tough one. I am not a passive personality, but many times I have felt unequipped to deal with my daughters. We must remember that God is using our mothering experience to work in us the things that need to be changed. The personality of the child God gave you is no accident. God wants to use it to strengthen your—and your child's—weaknesses.

Sometimes a mom resorts to emotional manipulation so she doesn't have to face the issue and can still get a limited amount of obedience from her child. She doesn't want her child to grow up and have his own life; so she keeps him dependent on her by not teaching him responsibility and not letting him experience life's consequences. Or she may play the part of the weak woman who needs her children to care for her. Passive-aggressive behavior can be an effective tool for manipulating her children to do what she wants.

The personality of the child God gave you is no accident. God wants to use it to strengthen your—and your child's—weaknesses.

I have seen moms who, for whatever reason, have given up on fighting for the important stuff but who make a huge fuss over the little stuff. The kids are confused about why their mom is losing it over the towel that isn't hung straight in the bathroom but doesn't care what time they come home at night. Let's get our motives pure and right. And let's not substitute unhealthy manipulation for healthy confrontation.

This mom thing is not about me. That is, it's not about getting my emotional needs met. It's not about being able to say I'm the best mom. It's not about my being right or popular. It's about raising these kids to be responsible, mature, and godly. Sure, we need to have our needs met, but not through our parenting. Parenting is all about doing what is best for our kids.

The Benefits of Boundaries

Boundaries benefit our children. We need to know that and believe it so we will be prepared for the heat of battle when we are tempted to drop our boundaries.

Let's get our motives pure and right. And let's not substitute unhealthy manipulation for healthy confrontation.

Boundaries benefit our kids by helping them develop strong character and the ability to make good choices—invaluable assets that will stay with them through life. When we give our kids limits, they know how far they can safely go. It builds in them an inner sense of what is safe and not safe. It teaches them self-control.

We learn the powerful lesson of how boundaries benefit our kids from a priest named Eli and his two sons (1 Samuel 2:12–4:22). Eli and his sons were God's chosen priests to serve in his temple. In the books of Exodus through Deuteronomy, God gave specific directions on how the priests were to serve

God in the temple. However, Eli's sons did as they pleased. They weren't just slightly undependable; they were immoral, disobedient, and disrespectful to God. Word got to Eli of his sons' atrocities. He confronted them, but it only amounted to a scolding. They continued their wickedness. Finally, God had had enough. He spoke to the boy-prophet Samuel and told him that he was going to "judge [Eli's] family forever because of the sin he knew about; his sons made themselves contemptible, and he failed to restrain them" (3:13). Eli's sons and daughter-in-law died premature deaths by the hand of God.

I am not saying that God is going to punish us by killing us or our children, but we must learn that God is serious about parenting. Eli took the lazy, manipulative route. In 1 Samuel 2:22-25 he whined to his sons, "Why do you do such things? . . . It is not a good report that I hear spreading among the LORD's people." He stood there wringing his hands, saying in effect, "Why don't you boys be good? The neighbors are talking." Where was the backbone? As we see, his words were empty. Boundaries put power and meaning to our words. When boundaries are violated, we need to carry out the stated consequence.

 I am not saying that God is going to punish us by killing us or our children, but we must learn that God is serious about parenting.

One of the things that made my mom such an effective Queen Mom was that she was confident and didn't bend under our pressure. She never appeared to be upset by our challenges. She calmly and firmly stated the boundary and the consequence if that boundary were violated. That was it. We knew she meant what she said and she would carry through if we chose to test the borders. I never once thought my mom couldn't handle my disobedience. Too bad Eli couldn't have gotten some parenting advice from my mom!

Eli tried using guilt and his own embarrassment to get his sons to change their behavior. Another emotional weapon parents use on their children is withdrawal or detachment. The child disagrees with or challenges the parent, so the parent withdraws, thereby telling the child she is no longer loved. In their book *Boundaries*, Drs. Henry Cloud and John Townsend make this application, "The child translates that message something like this: *When I'm good, I am loved. When I'm bad, I am cut off.*"[2] How damaging is that to our kids? The doctors go on to further apply this principle: "When children feel parents withdrawing, they readily believe that they are responsible for Mom and Dad's feelings."[3] Is this what we want our kids to believe about us?

Parenting with emotional manipulation reaches far into every area of our children's lives, both present and future. Cloud and Townsend explain, "Children of parents like these grow up to be adults who are terrified that setting boundaries will cause severe isolation and abandonment."[4]

> When we teach our kids boundaries, we are not just teaching them to follow our rules and make good choices. We are teaching them to form their own boundaries.

Do you see the danger, moms? When we use emotional manipulation on our kids, we are teaching them it is dangerous and costly to disagree with others and set their own boundaries.

So they don't make choices that are good for them. We all know people who could not take a stand against someone else, so they are in a bad marriage; had a child out of marriage; let people take advantage of their generosity in finances, help, and possessions.

When we teach our kids boundaries, we are not just teaching them to follow our rules and make good choices. We are teaching them to form their own boundaries by knowing which people are good for them to be with, when they need to take care of their bodies (eat, exercise, rest), and when they need to take care of their emotional and spiritual health (get away from everyone, see friends, take time with the Lord). We do this by listening to our kids, asking leading questions, and making short, insightful comments.

Concerning Friends

One of our princesses had a friend who was going through a hard time with her parents' divorce and the custody arrangements. I listened to my daughter tell me about her friend. I showed her my concern for this little girl and let her know this was a difficult situation. My princess had already caught on that she couldn't be responsible for this friend's sadness. She told me, "I can't really relate to Sarah and that's OK. She talks to Brittany more because Brittany is going through the same thing." Our princess has learned that we can't take on the problems of our friends. We care, but we can't magically fix them.

Another one of our girls learned the lesson of challenging friends the hard way. She became good friends with a girl. Eventually the girl started relationships with kids who did not have the same values as the girl's family or our princess. The girl adopted the negative attitudes and actions of her new friends. She tried to pursue our princess as a friend, but our princess learned the girl was not good for her and was even hurtful to her. So our daughter limited the time she spent with her and didn't let this friend's comments penetrate her heart.

I applauded Princess Two for her insight and courage to do what was best for both of them. The friend was hurtful to my daughter. It wouldn't have been helpful to the friend had my daughter let this friend continue to put her down. The friend needed to learn that she can't treat people badly and still call them friends.

> I am amazed at the pace and intensity at which some kids live, and many do so by the decree of their queens.

Another vital boundary for our kids to learn concerns their social limits. We all have different social needs, and we must help our kids learn what is right for them. Princess Two is highly social, but she knows when she has had enough of her peers. One weekend I told her she could have friends over if she wanted to. Her reply perfectly expressed her feelings: "I have been with those kids all week. I need a break." Amen to that. Her week had been draining, and she knew her social limits.

Concerning Commitments

I am amazed at the pace and intensity at which some kids live, and many do so by the decree of their queens. Kids need to know it's OK to set limits on their commitments, and they need to learn how to do so. Evaluating their commitments helps them know what they can and can't handle.

At one time we hosted music lessons in our home. A college student came to our house and taught one of our girls and a few kids from school. One student in particular arrived at our house exhausted week after week. She had told our daughter how her week was full of lessons, practices, and activities. One day she looked as if she were going to pass out. I offered her a couple of cookies. She inhaled them. I asked if she would like a slice of the roast I'd made for supper. She ate the meat and a dinner roll with immense appreciation. She was astonished that we had homemade food for supper and ate together most nights. Her family's schedule would never allow that luxury. I got the impression that this girl had no choice in her schedule. She looked as if she wanted to jump off her not-so-merry-go-round life.

  She was astonished that we had homemade food for supper and ate together most nights.

Remember Princess Two's never-ending marching band season? She decided the time commitment wasn't worth what she was getting out of it. So her senior year she decided not to participate in marching band. She took her last year of high school to try other opportunities that weren't so demanding and that she previously hadn't had time for.

. . . .

Our kids need us to put boundaries in place to protect and train them physically, emotionally, and spiritually. When we do this appropriately, not using emotional control, we set in motion a chain of events in which our kids will learn to think and relate actions to their corresponding consequences. Then they will be more secure because their world is protected by firm boundaries and doesn't teeter on a mom's delicate emotions. Feeling secure will cause your children to be more confident in setting good personal boundaries that will keep them from making bad life choices. This type of parenting gives our kids a foundation for an abundant life—the life God planned for them.

So decide on your boundaries, giving your child the space to be who God made him to be. This will be an ongoing process for each child as he grows. Help your child find the boundaries that define who he is. Then determine to defend those boundaries.

You may not have had good role models for setting boundaries. You may have been parented with emotional manipulation. Admit that now. It's not being dishonoring to your parents. It's just telling the Lord that you now know the truth—and that you're ready to turn away from the lies you believed and receive his truth on being the mom he made you to be.

Royal Decree

Start today. Your past has not determined your future. God will honor us when we live to honor him. We *can* change the direction and style of our parenting. "I can do everything with the help of Christ who gives me the strength I need" (Philippians 4:13, *NLT*). You can do this!

Royal Inquiry

1. Would you agree that boundaries are good for our children? Why or why not?

2. Do you give your child clear boundaries, with consequences in the event those boundaries are violated? If no, can you identify with any of the inappropriate motives that keep moms from setting boundaries?

3. Can you admit that parenting is for your kids and not for your needs to be met? Will you let this truth guide your parenting? What changes will you make?

4. Do you allow your child to set his or her own healthy boundaries? Or do you, for example: insist on a hug or kiss when you (or a family member or friend) want one? insist he participate in activities that aren't in his area of talent just so you can have a "well-rounded" child? insist he keep relationships that are hurtful or harmful to him?

chapter seven

The Home May Be a Man's Castle, but It Is Mom's Domain!

The Importance and How-to of a Homey Home

Situations of disobedience and defiance arose more and more often with the prince and princess. However, the kingdom was growing and so were the demands on the king and queen. They had less time and energy for the prince and princess. Many times the king and queen gave in and let the children have their way to make up for the long hours their parents were in the court.

The king and queen in our fairy tale are missing the point. What is the benefit of ruling successfully in the world if the castle is in a state of anarchy? The queen hasn't made her home life a priority, and her children are feeling the effects and acting out because of it.

Moms are the heart of the home. In fact, we set the mood in the home. We keep communication flowing in our families. We provide a safe, comfortable haven for our families. We are crucial to the health of the home. Managing the home is one of the most important things we will ever do.

My girls love to see me spread my wings and take opportunities in my speaking ministry, but they don't enjoy having me gone. I am the heart that keeps the family functioning properly.

Gene is a great husband and father, but when I leave he reverts to his days as a U.S. Marine. He doesn't make the girls do one hundred jumping jacks before bed or scrub the bathroom with a toothbrush, but his focus becomes a mission—supper, dishes, homework, piano practice . . . He resembles Navy SEAL Lt. Shane Wolf, the main character in the movie *The Pacifier*. Lt. Wolf has a mission to fulfill—protecting the children of the Plummer family while their recently widowed mother goes on a trip to ensure national security. The Plummer kids soften his stern edges while Lt. Wolf keeps his motto "My way, no highway option" intact. And while Lt. Wolf—and Gene—do a great job with the house and kids, both families rejoice when mom returns home.

> OK, I feel like a failure when I compare myself with the Proverbs 31 woman, but that doesn't mean I shouldn't use her as my role model.

God tells us the importance of our role in the home: "Older women must train the younger women to love their husbands and their children, to live wisely and be pure, to take care of their homes, to do good, and to be submissive to their husbands. Then they will not bring shame on the word of God" (Titus 2:4, 5, *NLT*). What a powerful payoff. When we fulfill our role as queen of the home, we will not bring shame on the Word of God but, rather, glory to God. We will be giving people a reason to hear God's Word, because they will see its results in our families.

A Biblical Role Model

No better example of Queen Mom is given than in Proverbs 31. OK, I feel like a failure when I compare myself with the Proverbs 31 woman, but that doesn't mean I shouldn't use her as my role model. If I used that faulty philosophy toward the whole Word of God—*I fall short so why try?*—I wouldn't read the Word or try to live the righteous life. God gave us Proverbs 31 as a goal. We will never arrive, but here we have guidelines to help us in making decisions when it comes to our families and homes.

> Since families were instituted by God, Satan targets the home. He wants to destroy anything of God's, and that includes your family.

So what does this template look like? Her description begins, "Who can find a virtuous wife? For her worth is far above rubies" (Proverbs 31:10, *NKJV*). The footnote in the *NKJV* defines "virtuous" as "valor"—a wife of valor. *Valor* means "courage and boldness, as in battle; bravery."[1] Wow! Moms, we are called to courage and boldness as we battle for our families. And we *are* in a battle for our families, aren't we? Since families were instituted by God, Satan targets the home. He wants to destroy anything of God's, and that includes your family. We are called to defend and protect our families—our kingdoms. Being the reigning queen will take courage, boldness, and bravery.

Let's look at this incredible Proverbs 31 woman and see how we can use what we know about her as a template. In the last chapter we talked about the value of giving our kids room to be the persons God designed them to be. The same is true for moms. Since God made us all different—different personalities, situations, talents, resources—he created us equipped to become the moms he planned us to be. The key is to learn to be God's woman God's way; and to do that, we need to know God's Word and live it. How does that play out in some specific areas of your life and home?

Royal Threads

Read Proverbs 31:13, 19, 21, and 22, and you'll see how important clothes are to you and your home. Clothes express who we are and give us a sense of self-esteem. Princess Three had one outfit laid out on her bed this morning; but when she came out to breakfast, she was wearing something different. I asked what happened to the first outfit.

Learn to be God's woman God's way; and to do that, we need to know God's Word.

"I just have to be in the right mood to wear that sweater. This is more comfy for today." Since today is her birthday, how could I argue? She was comfy in her clothes. They expressed what she was feeling today—a relaxed, carefree, it's-my-day attitude. Her outfit was an outflow of who she is. She is free to express herself in the safe atmosphere of home.

Giving careful attention to your family's clothing communicates that you care and are invested in them. Since I have all girls,

I have given many hours in search of the perfect pair of jeans, prom dress, and pair of shoes. We aren't slaves to the trendy stores, but I do try to help the girls find stylish, appropriate clothes at a good price. Just recently a secondhand store opened near the mall. Its specialty is gently worn, trendy teen clothes. The princesses think they have found Heaven on earth—trendy clothes at a tiny fraction of the original price!

Even though most boys aren't into fashion the way girls can be, boys eventually reach an age when they do care. Take the time to help them find their look. But don't be shocked when it's a huge change from the clothes you picked out for them.

Giving careful attention to your family's clothing communicates that you care and are invested in them.

The family's appearance communicates volumes to the world. It tells people we love our families enough to make sure they look nice. It gives us credibility with a world that is searching for meaning; if we can appropriately clothe our families and ourselves, maybe we have it together enough to have answers to serious life questions.

If I wore my writing attire (old stretched-out turtleneck, faded jeans, and fake-suede slippers spotted with drops of coffee) when I took the platform to speak, you probably wouldn't give me a listen. However, when I step to the speaker's platform wearing a dressy pair of slacks, three-quarter-length jacket and a triple-string pearl necklace, you are more likely to believe I know what I'm talking about. I have credibility with you before I say one word.

My friend Erin shared with me a perfect example of this. She had a conversation with her daughter's teacher, a young woman who doesn't know the Lord. The teacher told Erin she knew there was something distinctive about her because Erin always had her act together. She found Erin intriguing because she is different from the other moms, and the teacher wanted to learn what made Erin different. Erin is what I consider a cool young mom. She has a fun, laid-back personality, and she dresses in a casual, chic style with a layered haircut that requires a little blow-drying to style it. Her husband is in full-time ministry, so they don't have a big clothing budget. Erin is a smart sale shopper and is attentive to the styles, doing her best to stay current without being too trendy. Even though she has two young children and is pregnant with a third child, she takes a few minutes to do her makeup.

The world is watching us, and we need to be dressed and ready.

> If you haven't updated your look in a couple of years, or if you're wearing your hair the way you did in high school or college, please get some help!

I love the part in *The Princess Diaries 2: Royal Engagement* when Princess Mia has arrived at the castle to begin her duties as Princess of Genovia. Queen Clarisse is giving her a tour of her living quarters. The princess and queen step into the closet (which is the size of my living room), and Queen Clarisse opens door after door to reveal the princess's new royal wardrobe—numerous gorgeous, perfectly matched, and accessorized outfits!

Our woman of valor in Proverbs 31 is described as wearing clothes fit for royalty. The *Amplified Bible* describes her clothes as being "of linen, pure and fine, and of purple [such as that of which the clothing of the priests and the hallowed cloths of the temple were made]" (v. 22). As we'll see later, she was good with finances, so she wasn't running up the charge cards in order to look nice. She wore the best she could afford, and because she was in tune with her family and her world, she knew what looked appropriate. She kept up on fashion without being a slave to it.

If you haven't updated your look in a couple of years, or if you're wearing your hair the way you did in high school or college, please get some help! This can be done inexpensively and without a lot of effort.

Since I am not the queen of a country, I cannot afford Princess Mia's wardrobe. However, I have learned the art of buying several quality pieces (almost always on sale) that coordinate with each other. I buy inexpensive, trendy accessories to update my look. This strategy gives me many fresh looks without investing a lot of time and money. I also get fashion updates from catalogs, the national morning news programs, and the fashion segments on TV programs like *Oprah*. See what they're showing and decide what look is right for you.

Do you have a friend who is up on the latest and whom you can trust for help? Updating your look will be a bit scary, but you won't regret it. I'm sure under that vintage look is a fabulous, cool, confident, and dare I say, sexy woman. Let her out! Your husband will be so impressed.

Royal Eats

Our Proverbs 31 woman of valor knew the importance of providing good food for her family. She is described as being "like the merchant ships, bringing her food from afar" (v. 14). After my grocery shopping trips (many times needing two carts to get the groceries to the car), I feel like a merchant ship bringing food from afar. This is such a vital part of our role in creating a place of refuge for our families. Food is the universal language of hospitality. One of the most important aspects of the festivals in the Old Testament was food. And Jesus spent numerous good times around his friends' tables. Food says, "Come in, relax, let's talk."

After the girls have had a hard day at school, I want to welcome them home and help them relax, so I have snacks available for them. Some days I have cookies fresh from the oven. (It's not hard—you can do it too. The refrigerated, ready-to-bake cookie dough is a great, time-saving option.) A bowl of fruit is on the breakfast bar, or they can survey the pantry and fridge to find whatever appeals to them—graham crackers, pretzels, marshmallows, cereal, yogurt, juice . . . And the most important component of this after-school snackfest is that while they are chatting about the day, I am taking it in and offering support and encouragement. This special time between my princesses and me has yielded much benefit!

Take time to grocery shop for your family and serve food in an atmosphere of love, giving your family your full attention.

This type of relationship building works on guys too. As I previously mentioned, at one time we had a college student come to our home to give music lessons to one of our girls and some other kids. I started a habit of having hot-from-the-oven cookies and cold milk for him while he waited for the kids to arrive. It was so fun to watch him devour close to a dozen cookies and a couple of glasses of milk in a few minutes. He talked about his day, his plans, his girlfriend (who became his fiancée), his wedding plans, and marriage jitters. One day while sitting at the bar having his snack, he said, "This is the best part of my week." We built relationship with this young man over a few cookies and a couple gallons of milk. How hard was that?

Food gives us a reason to sit and talk. Serve whatever works for your family. One of my friends doesn't care for baked goodies, so she served her teen boys nachos and quesadillas. These were quickly made with inexpensive ingredients. One of my daughter's guy friends loved mixing a jar of salsa with a jar of cheese sauce and then microwaving it as dip for tortilla chips.

The type of food isn't the issue. What's important is that you take time to grocery shop for your family and serve food in an atmosphere of love, giving your family your full attention. It's called being available. My friends will tell you in unison that from three o'clock on is my time with my family. Sure, I will take a call, but I won't chat long. My time with my family is precious. It is when I do my parenting and relationship building.

Proverbs 31:15 continues, "She gets up while it is still dark; she provides food for her family and portions for her servant girls." Remember, this is a template—don't freak out. The idea here is to provide meals for your family. With a meal, the family will feel your love, your connection with them.

If you're not a morning person, you may cringe at the idea of getting up "while it is still dark." I have a great memory of visiting my grandma. As I lay in bed at night trying to go to sleep, I heard her setting the table for breakfast. My grandma was not a morning person, but my grandpa had to leave for work early.

So Grandma was creative; she set the table for breakfast the night before. That way she didn't have to get organized in the morning; she only had to plug in the coffeepot and fry his eggs.

Could we get creative too? How could you prepare ahead to have some breakfast and time for your family? Set out the dishes the night before? How about having juice boxes or individual yogurts handy in the fridge? What would your family like? What can you do to make it happen? Mostly, your family would probably like a little bit of you too.

Royal Funds

This Bible woman of valor was good with her money. Ouch. Touchy subject, I know, but I didn't bring it up; God did. Proverbs 31 says, "She considers a field and buys it; out of her earnings she plants a vineyard" (v. 16). Evidently, she had a home business as well, according to verse 24: "She makes belted linen garments and sashes to sell to the merchants" (*NLT*). What can we learn from this woman's example? She gave thought and planning to her finances. Each family will have its own plan for how they handle the money. In our family, I pay the bills and do the banking. Gene handles our investments and taxes. It works for us. The main point is, the woman of valor responsibly handles the money in her care.

Nothing can ruin the harmony of a home faster than a fight about money. I encourage you to be wise with what you have. Shop smart for groceries, clothes, and furniture. When we use money wisely, we can have what we need for our families. The Lord will reward our efforts.

If you have no idea how to make a family budget or how to get out of your financial mess, contact an adviser. Crown Financial Ministries (www.crown.org) offers resources that have helped countless families put their finances in order and thereby get rid of the stress that comes with financial problems.

Royal Strength

The Proverbs 31 mom wasn't a slacker. "She sets about her work vigorously; her arms are strong for her tasks. She sees that her trading is profitable, and her lamp does not go out at night" (vv. 17, 18). It takes work to keep our homes comfortable and stay in touch relationally. Lots of work. This may be an area of weakness for you. We all have weaknesses. The apostle Paul talks about his weaknesses in 2 Corinthians 12:9, 10: "[Jesus] said to me, 'My grace is sufficient for you, for my power is made perfect in weakness.' Therefore I will boast all the more gladly about my weaknesses, so that Christ's power may rest on me. That is why, for Christ's sake, I delight in weaknesses, in insults, in hardships, in persecutions, in difficulties. For when I am weak, then I am strong."

 The Proverbs 31 mom wasn't a slacker. "She sets about her work vigorously."

Take your area of weakness to Jesus and ask for his strength and guidance. Then get up and do what he says. He won't miraculously clean your kitchen (though he could!). We must do the work, but we do it in Jesus' power, not in our own.

I am not a slave to our home. It is clean enough for anyone to drop by anytime, but it is not perfect. As I previously mentioned, the girls and I clean on Saturday mornings. Through the week everyone is responsible for keeping her stuff picked up. This plan keeps the house, as Donna Otto says, "comfortable for us."

Donna's book *Secrets to Getting More Done in Less Time* changed the way I cared for our home and the way I organized myself, my paperwork, finances, and schedule. The book is full of practical ideas to get your home organized and running smoothly. I don't do everything she suggested, but I chose what worked for me.[2] Now I follow my plan for housecleaning and don't give the house another thought for the week. The same goes for the laundry, bill paying, and kids' schedules.

> Being a mom isn't for wimps. I'm not talking personality; I'm talking attitude.

One year on vacation I found a combination planner and wallet. It was imitation red leather, so of course, I fell in love with it. It makes my life so much easier. Everything I need to know is in the planner part (Donna covers this), and everything money related is in the wallet part. I throw this in my purse on the way out the door, and I am ready for anything from a trip to the emergency room to a shopping day. Working my plan is freeing . . . and it gives me time to write a book!

Royal Attitude

The woman of valor definitely has attitude. Proverbs 31:25 says, "She is clothed with strength and dignity; she can laugh at the days to come." She has confidence. Being a mom isn't for wimps. I'm not talking personality; I'm talking attitude. It shows through in our character, perseverance, convictions, and determination.

If you want to exert a positive influence on the atmosphere of your home, you need to be strong. The Hebrew root of the word *strong,* as used in this Scripture, means to be "stout."[3] Webster defines *stout* as "courageous, strong, sturdy, and firm." We become stout through our relationship with the Lord and from the strength of our convictions. As we develop God's vision for our families and form the plan to help get them there, we will become passionate—which will fuel our strength. Nothing dare get in our way.

The Proverbs 31 wonder woman also is covered in dignity. She knows the importance of her role, and she takes it seriously. This doesn't mean she is always serious, but she brings dignity to her role as Queen Mom. She doesn't trash-talk, and she doesn't tolerate trash talk from others.

We love to laugh in our house, and no one loves to let out a roar more than I do. Just last night I laughed so hard I had to catch my breath. In our recreation room Kerry had built a fort out of cardboard boxes. Somehow, I'm not quite sure how, Gene's reading chair was put behind one of the cardboard walls. Gene didn't care; he only wanted a quiet place to read, so he sat down there. When Kelsey and I came into the room, Kelsey took one look at her dad (sitting with his profile toward us) and said, "Doesn't it look like Dad is sitting in a box?" It did! The box came up to his chin, and his legs stuck out from the side. It looked like Gene was sitting in the box reading. How hilarious! I doubled over in laughter—it doesn't take much to entertain me!

We know what is appropriate to laugh about and what crosses the line. The kids are not allowed to be disrespectful to the king and me or to each other. The same goes for the king and me; we aren't disrespectful to the kids. We need to be careful not to put our kids down or embarrass them, especially in front of others.

I concede I will inevitably and inadvertently embarrass our kids—especially when they are between the ages of thirteen and sixteen, when our very existence is an embarrassment to them. And although my girls don't worry that I will purposely say something to embarrass them in front of their friends, I have been known to expose my lack of techy knowledge or pop culture savvy. They roll their eyes and laugh. What can I say? I'm old.

But I'm not talking about that sort of thing. I'm cautioning against comments that are inappropriate or meant to embarrass. Things like sharing their secrets, dreams, shortcomings, or personal and physical issues. This tears at their self-esteem and angers them toward us. God addresses this: "Fathers, do not provoke or irritate or fret your children [do not be hard on them or harass them], lest they become discouraged and sullen and morose and feel inferior and frustrated [Do not break their spirit.]" (Colossians 3:21, *AMP*).

  When we are reigning as Queen Mom, we exude confidence, and that gives the home an atmosphere of safety, security, and comfort.

Another way the Queen Mom is clothed with dignity is that she behaves like the queen when the kids have friends over or when she is with her children's friends elsewhere. Moms make a huge mistake and embarrass their kids when they try to dress like teens and try to be friends with their children's friends. Remember, you had your chance at youth. You're the adult now; act like it. Sure, we can talk with these young people and get to know them. But we do this as the mother, not like a teenager.

Royal Confidence
When we are reigning as Queen Mom, we exude confidence,

and that gives the home an atmosphere of safety, security, and comfort. Our woman of valor is ready for anything. "She laughs with no fear of the future" (v. 25, *NLT*).

Whoa. Is she nuts or superspiritual or what? Since she is our biblical template, I must rule out nuts. Superspiritual seemed reasonable; but again, because she is our role model, this characteristic of hers must be attainable. So I must also rule out superspiritual. This woman can laugh at the future with no fear because of her confidence in the Lord. She has trusted the Lord in tough situations and found that he's never deserted her (Joshua 1:5) and has always taken care of her (Psalm 55:22). She can laugh because she knows the future can't bring anything that she can't handle with the Lord. "Blessed is the man who trusts in the Lord, whose confidence is in him. He will be like a tree planted by the water that sends out its roots by the stream. It does not fear when heat comes; its leaves are always green. It has no worries in a year of drought and never fails to bear fruit" (Jeremiah 17:7, 8).

During a friend's birthday party, a small group of us sat in the corner with our coffee and shared the bloody battles we were fighting. Hard stuff—like grown kids making poor choices, a dying spouse, raising teens, and financial difficulties. We wondered with each other, *Will our lives ever get any easier? Will we ever have a time when something doesn't try to steal our sleep and our peace?* We decided no. But the crucial thing is that we have learned through everything we are experiencing that God is always with us, always providing, always comforting, always enabling us to do the next thing. We have learned that God is faithful. He gives us the confidence to laugh at the future.

That confidence lights up your home with stability and comfort and gives your little royals a place where they can share their fears—because they know you can handle it.

A Biblical Challenge

There's one final description of the Proverbs 31 woman of valor: "She carefully watches all that goes on in her household and does not have to bear the consequences of laziness" (v. 27, *NLT*). We are it. Queen Moms are the keepers of the family. We know who's doing what, how they are feeling, what they are feeling, and when something isn't quite right.

To carefully watch all that goes on in our families, we can't be lazy. And we need to be available for our families—emotionally and physically—as much as we can. Yes, we all need time for ourselves, but we need to arrange our schedules to reflect our priorities. Does your schedule reflect that your family is a top priority? Deal with phone calls, paperwork, and computer work when it won't interfere with communicating with your family. Even if your kids and husband aren't especially verbal, be available. Save your mindless work to do when they are home so they know you can be easily interrupted.

I realize many single moms and moms who work outside the home don't have much time at home, but you can make some changes to create an atmosphere that says "I'm here for you." Tell your family you want to be more available and involved; then give them permission to interrupt when they need you. Now it's up to you to show them you meant what you said.

• •

Many women today seem to feel trapped or powerless or unimportant. But moms need never feel like that when they rule their castles God's way.

Royal Decree

Proverbs 31:30 says, "A woman who fears the Lord is to be praised." The woman of valor had a living, personal relationship with the Lord. Your relationship with God will give you everything you need to be the queen your family needs. Take one step today to further develop your friendship with God.

Royal Inquiry

1. What is the single most important thing you're doing right now to manage your home well?

2. Are you ready to be the woman of valor for your family? If no, what issues are in your way? Take them to the Lord.

3. Look at the different characteristics in the woman of valor template. Where are you doing well? Where do you need help? List some practical ways you can improve in these areas. Sometimes we need a friend to help us in an area where we are weak, and we can help her in her area of weakness.

4. If you haven't committed to a daily time with God, will you do so now? Without the Lord, we can't successfully meet what life demands. What practical steps do you need to take to guard this time alone with him?

chapter eight

Threats from Other Kingdoms

Resisting Mommy Peer Pressure

The king and queen didn't want to make the prince and princess angry. They wanted the prince and princess to always like them. They could take away privileges, but that seemed mean. They could ground the prince and princess, but then they would have to stay home and spend time with them. Other kings and queens didn't spend time at home with their children. What would people think of the king and queen if they missed the upcoming ball so they could stay at home with their children?

How can the queen in *The Kingdom* fairy tale be such a confident leader in the outside world when she can't be strong against peer pressure in her parenting? A quick look around the next school event or church program you attend will reveal a number of moms who are successes in their careers, yet they are directionless in their parenting. Their own lack of purpose leaves them easily influenced by what everyone else is doing.

Have I mentioned that I'm a control freak? Usually this is a weakness to be improved upon, but in the role of Queen Mom, it gives me the edge. I have definite ideas about how I want to do the mom thing. I am alert to anything that comes into our kingdom that could interfere with my sovereign plan. This is not to say that it's my way or the highway. I prefer to think of myself as airport security (only more loving, sensitive, and efficient).

When an unfamiliar influence tries to gain entry into our castle, it is stopped at the security check by the queen herself. I take it through my priority and convictions checklists. If I don't have enough information to make a ruling, I search and inquire to get the necessary information. If the unfamiliar influence is deemed positive, it passes and is welcomed into the castle. If the unfamiliar influence is deemed negative, it is banned and given the official Queen Mom red flag.

> All the right priorities and convictions won't mean a thing in our kingdoms if we fail to stand against pressure from others to conform to ways which are against what we know to be true and right for our families.

Negative influences arise from the obvious sources—media, peers, celebrities, and entertainment choices—and also from familiar and friendly sources. The tricky part is in not only identifying the negative influences but also having the strength to resist them and stop them from affecting our families and decisions. This is where we may win or lose our kingdoms. All the right priorities and convictions won't mean a thing in our kingdoms if we fail to stand against pressure from others to conform to ways which are against what we know to be true and right for our families.

In the movie *The King and I*, Anna immediately engages the king in a battle of the wills over the house he promised her. It doesn't take the king long to see that she is as strong-willed as he is. He says, "You are not afraid of King. Not to be afraid is good thing."

We cannot be afraid to stand our ground regarding what God has called us to. When other mothers or teachers challenge the rules and boundaries we have for our kids, we must explain our convictions with calmness and respect. Sometimes the other party will agree with our convictions. But if not, graciously withdraw your child from the situation. To my knowledge, I have not made any enemies by standing my ground with dignity and kindness.

Know Your Priorities

Do you know your priorities and convictions? I hope our discussion thus far has stirred your thoughts toward making a mental draft of what might go on your list.

Here are my priorities:

- keeping my relationship with God daily, fresh, and honest
- giving my husband and my girls quality time and as much quantity time as I can when they are home (this includes staying on top of my home chores)
- serving God through my God-given passion
- spending time with my friends and extended family

It took several years for me to develop this list, and I hope to help you do it much faster. My life is so much simpler because I live by this list of priorities. I know what to say yes to and what to say no to—with no guilt. My convictions are based on God's Word and how I apply it to my life and my kids' lives. Since new situations were always coming up in each child's life, I often went to the Bible and wise Christian counsel for guidance. Many times, too, God gave me a mother's intuition or gut feeling that something wasn't right.

It's time for you to start getting real about your priorities and convictions. In our discussion, what has registered with you? What is important to you—no matter what your friends and family are doing or not doing? What plan is God showing you? I hope you started this list at the end of chapter 2. If you didn't, now is the time. It can seem overwhelming, but we have to start somewhere.

 I know what to say yes to and what to say no to—with no guilt. My convictions are based on God's Word and how I apply it.

If you could start tomorrow morning fresh with no previous commitments and only your family, how would you prioritize your life? How important is your family to you? How about your time with God? Now add serving the Lord, a job, extended family, and friends. Which of these would make the cut if you were starting fresh? Take a minute and think about it.

Let me show you how I apply the principle of priorities in my life and in decision making.

I am a person who needs eight hours of sleep a night, going to bed about the same time and getting up at the same time.

Years ago when God impressed upon me to get up at five thirty in the morning to meet with him, I trusted him for the energy to get up and to make it through my day. Now as I lie in bed at five thirty, wishing for a little more time, I realize that I won't be any more refreshed at six thirty than I am at five thirty. God is always faithful to give me what I need when I put him first.

Whenever I mention a morning time with the Lord, the night people comment, "You can say that because you're a morning person." I finally got a better understanding of night people the other day. Princess Three happened to get up early on a Saturday and joined me in the living room when I was having my quiet time. I suggested she get her Bible and devotional book and have her quiet time with me. She said, "I'd rather do it at night when I'm awake." OK, I get it. But if you say you will meet with the Lord at night, make it a commitment; and don't let life or fatigue crowd him out. We must *live* our priorities.

God is always faithful to give me what I need when I put him first.

What about your family? Where are they on your list of priorities? At the top, you say? Plug your family into your schedule. Do they fit? Think about the time away from your family that various opportunities will take. How many evenings do you want to be gone during a week or a month? What about the prep time for these commitments—how much time will that take from your family? If your family is a top priority, your choices and schedules will reflect it.

Please hear me. I'm not saying we should be chained to our homes. We'll have plenty of freedom and fulfillment when we understand God's plan for us.[1] You can make decisions accordingly—saying yes to what takes you in that direction (in line with your priorities) and saying no to the rest, even if it is good stuff. Now your schedule won't be crowded with activities that take you away from the important things in your life—your family and your calling.

I am privileged to be part of a once-a-month prayer group. This close group of friends meets over brunch to share, encourage, advise, and pray for each other. It is one of the best parts of my month. Since a couple of the members are teachers, the brunch is occasionally held on days off school. However, since my girls are out of school those days too, I must make a choice—go to prayer group and leave the girls at home or miss prayer group to be with my girls.

My decision is always clear—miss prayer group and spend the time with my girls. They are my preference; I see my friends at other times. My girls and I take this day off to enjoy together, usually by shopping and doing lunch out. Princess Two is in the last half of her junior year. My time with her is growing short. I don't want to miss any opportunities to enjoy her before she heads off to adulthood.

I have to say this to you straight: you *can't* do it all. The truth is that some of our schedules are ridiculous. No amount of prioritizing or reorganizing is going to help. You need to make some hard decisions and cut some activities. Work fewer hours. Volunteer less. Say no more often. "Do what is right and do not give way to fear" (1 Peter 3:6).

Defend Your Priorities

Now you have your priorities and convictions in order. Here comes the difficult part: defending them. To do that, we must know what we are defending them against. Who or what is our enemy? Ready? The enemy is one of us. At first glance she looks like a mild-mannered mom, but when she is overcome with the passion of accomplishing her agenda, she is transformed into a formidable, power-driven dictator. (Like Little Larry in the movie *Sky High*. Little Larry is a small-for-his-age, fourteen-year-old with red hair and glasses. But when his superhero powers transform him into a two-ton rock man, he is to be feared.)

I have to say this to you straight: you can't do it all. The truth is that some of our schedules are ridiculous. No amount of prioritizing or reorganizing is going to help. You need to make some hard decisions and cut some activities. Work fewer hours. Volunteer less. Say no more often. "Do what is right and do not give way to fear."

Have you met her? I have on several occasions. The following experience was the one that steeled my determination to defend my territory.

One day I was doing my thing at home when the phone rang. Innocently and cheerfully I answered, "Hello?"

"Hello, since your daughter is involved in this activity (will remain vague to protect involved parties, including myself), you have these choices of times to help out."

What?! Wait! I don't know anything about helping out. She's barely involved. All I could manage was, "Uh . . . well . . ."

"You do want to help, don't you?"

The truth? I'd rather give birth. "Well, what were my choices again?"

By now this other mom was losing patience with me because I did not respond with the same enthusiasm she'd brought into the phone call. She once again listed the jobs. I chose one that required the least amount of time and which allowed me to work alongside a good friend.

Later I told this friend of my phone conversation. She had impeccable insight: "Oh, she's like that because this is her fun. This is my fun too, but it's not everyone's fun."

That's it! This mom had *her* priorities, and she assumed that they would be mine also. Big mistake. Because not only was this activity *not* my priority, I know my priorities—and I will defend them. After two decades of being the Queen Mom, I'm not about to let another mom invade my kingdom by telling me how to spend my time.

This is why setting your priorities and plan is so important. It will give you direction and confidence when you are assaulted from all directions on a variety of issues by other moms who want a piece of you. They may try to influence you to be more liberal, to be more strict, to breastfeed or not, to have your child potty-trained by age two . . . or four . . . or whenever the child decides to, to homeschool . . . or send your child to public school . . . or to private school, to get you to go to their endless home parties, to volunteer on their endless committees, and to go to their endless meetings.

Not all your friends will share your priorities or child-rearing philosophy. Stand strong in your convictions and sweetly decline, keeping your friendship intact.

My friend Nancy had the following experience: The mom of her son's friend was going to be out of town and asked if the boy could stay at Nancy's. No problem, except for one issue. Nancy and her husband had decided that their young son would not be allowed to play with guns in warfare games. Hunting was fine, but they wanted to teach him to respect human life. The other boy's main imaginative play was with guns and shooting people. Nancy talked with the boy's mom (who was also Nancy's friend) and told her that her son was welcome but the guns would need to stay home. She went on to name all the toys and activities they had for the little guys. Her friend sweetly tried to change Nancy's mind because she didn't want her son to be upset. Nancy sweetly but firmly replied, "If that's not possible, we will wait until he's a little older to deal with the disappointment." The other mother ultimately agreed to Nancy's rules. Their friendship stayed strong and continues to grow because they respected each other's decisions.

 After two decades of being the Queen Mom, I'm not about to let another mom invade my kingdom by telling me how to spend my time.

Nancy and her husband handled this situation well. They had their priorities and convictions in place. They knew they did not want their young son playing with guns. They were not making a condemning statement about parents who let their kids play with guns. It was simply their conviction, and they defended it.

You are now firm in your priorities, and you have identified the enemy and her modus operandi. You are ready to resist one of the great influences in modern motherhood—mommy peer pressure.

Resist Peer Pressure

The other moms can't make us do what they want, make us

go against what we know to be right for our families. Millions of dollars have been spent in ad campaigns to encourage our kids to resist peer pressure. "Just say no." "Don't do drugs, stay in school." "Steer clear of pot." "Live above the influence." And with everything in us, we try to communicate to our kids the foolishness of giving in to peer pressure. Yet when we are engaged in mommy-to-mommy battle, we are fearful—even chicken—and all too often we give in to other moms.

Why is that? We don't want them to be mad at us. We don't want them to think we are lazy or uncaring. We can't defend our position. We want to be liked. We don't like confrontation.

Seeing those reasons in print helps us realize how silly and powerless they are. (We certainly think they're silly when our children give in for the same reasons, don't we?) We need to absorb some truth to give us the power to gracefully stand our ground and resist mommy peer pressure.

> **When we are engaged in mommy-to-mommy battle, we are fearful—even chicken—and all too often we give in to other moms.**

The Bible is full of promises of God's protection, strength, and wisdom. It is replete with real-life examples of God doing amazing things for regular people. Yet when we come up against another mom, our hearts beat faster, we start to stutter, and our convictions wilt. So how did these regular folks in the Bible become heroes of the Bible? They believed what God told them, and they acted on it. It's called faith and obedience. We can do the same. But we need to know what God says.

I love the apostle Paul's confident attitude: "It is required that those who have been given a trust must prove faithful. I care very little if I am judged by you or by any human court; indeed, I do not even judge myself" (1 Corinthians 4:2, 3). We have been given a huge trust—our children. We must prove to be faithful to raise them and be the Queen Mom as God directs us, not following the whims of the other moms. I especially love verse 3. *The Message* puts it in today's language: "It matters very little to me what you think of me, even less where I rank in popular opinion. I don't even rank myself. Comparisons in these matters are pointless." If Paul doesn't care what people think, why should we be distracted from our mission by others' opinions? This is especially true when the "others" are not believers.

> "It matters very little to me what you think of me, even less where I rank in popular opinion. I don't even rank myself. Comparisons in these matters are pointless."

Here's an e-mail I received from one of my dear friends:

When Megan was between two and two-and-a-half years old and having a very difficult time speaking and communicating, we were at the school to pick up her brother, and she had a fit about something. She couldn't tell me what the problem was or what she wanted, so she screamed and cried and had a fit (but not a tantrum). I did not spank or discipline Megan for not being able to communicate. Two other mothers were nearby, and one mother rolled her eyes.

The next day when we were in a group of ladies, the

mother who had rolled her eyes made a point of saying how when her youngest son has a fit, she spanks him and puts him to bed. It was pointed at me and I realized that. I was extremely embarrassed, almost to the point of tears. It was a real holier-than-thou attitude. . . . I was very angry because this mother was unaware of Megan's problem.

I stewed about it for a week until the Holy Spirit said to me, 'Why does it matter what SHE thinks?!' After that point, I decided that I really only needed to be accountable to God and [my husband] for how I handle and deal with my kids. This woman either did not know of Megan's problem or was unaware of the degree to which Megan could not communicate to us. Even if she had not known about Megan's difficulty, I didn't feel like I needed to explain myself to this lady. At a certain point I had to MAKE THE DECISION that what she thought really did not matter. After that incident, I felt a huge burden lifted off my shoulders.[2]

Don't Be a People Pleaser

Being a people pleaser is not for the Queen Mom. Living to please others is against God's plan for us. In the book of Galatians, Paul stresses what drives him: "Obviously, I'm not trying to be a people pleaser! No, I am trying to please God. If I were still trying to please people, I would not be Christ's servant" (Galatians 1:10, *NLT*). You go, Paul! Why are we trying to be people pleasers?

In Proverbs 29:25 we are told, "Fear of man will prove to be a snare, but whoever trusts in the LORD is kept safe." Not only is trying to please people pointless, it is a snare—something that will lure us, entangle us, and trap us. But when we trust

God (by being the Queen Mom his way), we are kept safe (we are under his sovereign protection). When we are trying to be people pleasers, we are not trusting God. He may not protect us from the negative consequences that come with that.

Nancy and her friend did not let the fear of each other's rejection get in the way of dealing with their situation in a mature way. Neither took offense. The friend respected Nancy's house rules, thereby teaching her own son that he can't have his way all the time. When he is in someone else's house, he must obey their rules. The thing I really love here is that they not only kept their friendship, but even after several years, they are still growing as friends.

So many times moms let difficulties between their children negatively affect their relationship or even kill the friendship. We need to give our kids room to develop their personalities. Maybe our kids just won't be friends past a certain age. That's cool. They're changing and growing. We do the same thing—some friends we keep up with, and some friends go a different direction. Unless we are willing to lose a good friend, we need to put some distance between our kids' friendships and our friendships.

> When we are trying to be people pleasers, we are not trusting God. He may not protect us from the negative consequences that come with that.

The key to dealing with our friends correctly is motive. When we fear losing friends because they won't agree with us, we have the wrong motive. In order to consistently defend our convictions, we need to lay down our fear of losing our friends.

Paul explains the importance of a right motive: "Our purpose is to please God, not people. He is the one who examines the motives of our hearts" (1 Thessalonians 2:4, *NLT*). What is your purpose? Do you want to please God or to please people? Be truthful—God already knows "the motives of our hearts." If your friend is truly a good friend, she will respect your position.

Be Gracious

The Queen Mom is gracious. Since Nancy was confident in her conviction, she was able to handle the conversation graciously when the issue of guns came up. How we communicate is so important. Nothing shuts down communication faster than someone ranting about her point of view.

 "Whatever happens, conduct yourselves in a manner worthy of the gospel of Christ."

In the 2004 presidential race, Howard Dean was a Democratic front-runner until, at a post-caucus rally, he belted out the names of states, punctuated with a "Yee-ha!" That sound bite gave the American people an unpresidential impression of Mr. Dean. He wasn't poised and stable. He didn't control his emotions, so people stopped listening. If we want to be heard, understood, and have a favorable outcome, we need a gracious, yet firm, posture. We can do it, and we can do it in a way that glorifies God. The Bible tells us, "Whatever happens, conduct yourselves in a manner worthy of the gospel of Christ" (Philippians 1:27).

I love watching Condoleezza Rice in action. On March 9, 2006, she was giving testimony about the war in Iraq at the Senate

Appropriations Committee. She was interrupted by a protester directly behind her. He shouted, "Blood is on your hands!" and "How many of you have children going to war?" While the man was removed, she remained calm and cool and continued her testimony. She conducted herself in a manner worthy of her Lord. Our challenge is to do the same.

• •

Determine your priorities. Determine to defend them. With a goal of pleasing the Lord, you'll find that mommy peer pressure will become less intimidating.

Royal Decree

This chapter may be where you win or lose your throne. You must defend your kingdom even against those who appear to be your allies. I have found that this battle draws me closer to Jesus, for he is sometimes the only one who understands all my circumstances. He had many experiences of standing alone while doing what God told him to do, and he will be faithful to give you the strength you need.

Royal Inquiry

1. Be real with yourself and God concerning your priorities and convictions. What things in your life need to go? If you can't bear to think about it, ask your husband or a trusted, mature friend.

2. What will you do about the areas that are stealing from your family and God's plan for you all?

3. What is the trigger that makes you cave in to other moms? Deal with it. Develop a posture to use during the next mommy peer pressure attack.

4. Do you struggle with being a people pleaser? Be truthful. Confess your struggle to God.

5. Did any of the Bible verses in this chapter grab your heart? Write them down on index cards and meditate on them— swallowing them like a strong antibiotic to fight the germs of mommy peer pressure.

6. Maybe the friends in your circle are not going to understand or respect your new priorities and convictions. Take it to Jesus. Ask him for one or two like-minded friends who can encourage you.

chapter nine

What Cool Queen Moms Know That We Don't

Majors, Minors, and Knowing the Difference

They decided that the best way to keep peace in their kingdom would be to give the prince and princess whatever they desired. The king and queen would do whatever they asked. Surely the prince and princess would eventually get tired of all this, and the king and queen would get their thrones back.

Our king and queen may be doing a great job as rulers, but they are doing so at the expense of their children. In the raising of their children, they don't know what's important and what's not, so they miss great opportunities to teach and train their prince and princess.

One day I heard myself saying, "You bought *that* to wear to school? And where did you get it?"

I couldn't believe what I was seeing. One of our princesses had gone to the secondhand store to buy clothes—actual clothes to be worn in public. These weren't the "gently worn" last year's fashions that secondhand stores are famous for. No, these clothes were old T-shirts with things like "Park District T-Ball 2000" written on them. These clothes were like the ones I take to the secondhand store because no one in our family will wear them! Forget the stylish clothes we had bought. Princess One wanted to wear someone else's obviously old shirts to school. I freaked out.

Who had lost her mind here—mother or child? I hate to admit it, but the answer was mother. I had forgotten the rules for majoring on the majors and minoring on the minors, aka being the cool Queen Mom. These rules have to do with keeping a growing relationship with your child and keeping perspective.

Rule One: Develop and Keep a Growing Relationship with Your Kids

Your relationship with your children is the linchpin in every area of their lives. I cannot say it strongly enough, so I will let Joe White say it: "Being an effective spiritual mentor to your teen [*I would add "child"*] begins with a strong parent-child relationship. Without that, you can do nothing. *The relationship is everything.* Write it down! Even when an awkward adolescent veneer says, 'I'm on my own now, and I don't need you,' the relationship is everything!"[1]

Princess One wanted to wear someone else's obviously old shirts to school. I freaked out.

God is the perfect example of pursuing and developing relationship with those who don't pursue a relationship with him. After God created Adam and Eve, he blessed them and gave them rule over the earth. In doing this he provided everything they needed for life. He took time to build relationship with them by meeting with them in the Garden of Eden. God showed Adam and Eve his love for them by building a relationship with them on their level (Genesis 1:27–2:25). After they sinned and tried to hide from God (3:8), he provided a way for them to continue in a relationship with him through animal sacrifice (Genesis 4:4, 5).

> God craves a relationship with us—his kids—so much that he was willing to give up everything precious to him to get it. Are we willing to do the same to have a relationship with <u>our</u> kids (even when they push us away)?

Later in history God lovingly built a relationship with his people Israel by providing for them, protecting them, delivering them, and guiding them—even though many times they were like bratty, ungrateful kids. Then when the time was right, he made the ultimate sacrifice to make a way for all people to have an intimate relationship with him. He sent Jesus from Heaven to earth to live a perfect life and then be tortured and killed as our atoning sacrifice. But that wasn't enough to get us in right relationship with God. Jesus not only died for our sins, he conquered death. God raised him from the grave on the third day, and now he sits at God's right hand on our behalf (1 Corinthians 15:20-23, 57; Acts 2:32, 33).

God craves a relationship with us—his kids—so much that he was willing to give up everything precious to him to get it. Are we willing to do the same to have a relationship with *our* kids (even when they push us away)? Are we willing to sacrifice our lifestyles, careers, ambitions, even ministry (I didn't say relationship with God!) to pursue a relationship with our kids?

This question needs to be answered honestly by stay-at-home moms as well as those who work outside the home. To have a vital relationship with our kids, we need to be there for them. If you are a stay-at-home mom, are you at home and attentive when your kids are home?

It breaks my heart to see some young moms treat their children simply as another material part of their lives.

For those moms who work outside the home but desire to be stay-at-home moms (and maybe even *ache* to be there), I want to quote from Larry Burkett's *Women Leaving the Workplace*: "The sad truth is that most working mothers sacrifice time with their families with little or nothing to show for it. Most of the average working mother's wages are consumed by taxes, transportation, child care costs, and clothing. Even when a working mother's income is large enough to substantially add to the family's budget, the surplus is often consumed by an expanded lifestyle."[2] Moms, you may want to reevaluate the "benefits" of your employment.

Ideally, our relationship building with our children should begin at their births. Sure, there will be a lot of work and sacrifice and heartache. But give yourself unconditionally to those babies. You cannot be an effective Queen Mom unless you do.

It breaks my heart to see some young moms treat their children simply as another material part of their lives. They carry their babies like they would a purse, or they drag their toddlers like a piece of pull-along luggage. They want to go do their thing—no matter what the needs of their children are. *Hey, isn't that what child care is for?* they think.

When that precious toddler begins to jabber and then talk and talk and talk, be an active listener. God listens to us while we jabber on about things he already knows. He delights in us (Zephaniah 3:17). When you are showing respect by listening and acknowledging your child's ideas, it helps build his self-esteem and creates a strong bond between the two of you. And he *can* tell when you are listening.

One day Kerry informed me, "Mom, I can tell when you're listening to me."

"Oh yeah. How?"

"When you're not listening, it takes you a while to answer me back."

Ouch. Keep listening through their elementary-school years, no matter how boring the topic of conversation may be. This will build the foundation of communication you desperately need for the junior high and senior high years.

A mom shared with me a shocking fact her teen daughter had told her: "Mom, none of the kids I know at school *[a Christian high school]* have any kind of relationship with their parents. They try to stay out of trouble so they won't have to talk to their parents." As Joe White said, "The relationship is everything!" Without it we have no influence in our kids' lives.

All of this communication shows you care and value your children. When they *believe* that you care and value them, you have the credibility you need to say and enforce the hard things. They know you are making decisions in their best interest, even though they may not be happy with your decisions. You have proven yourself through your acts of service, words of encouragement, and presence.

When Princess Two was a sophomore in high school, one of her teachers decided to show an R-rated movie to the class because of its social content. Permission slips were sent home. Gene checked out this movie on www.screenit.com. It took only a few seconds to realize this was not an appropriate film, as far as we were concerned; the negatives far outweighed the positives. We sent back the form, stating our objections and that our princess would not be viewing the film.

A couple of days later, the class discussion revolved mostly around why Princess Two was not going to watch the movie with the class. The other kids reacted with abhorrence that a parent would "interfere" with what a teen watched. To the teacher's credit, he honored our decision and stood behind our princess. This was a challenging time for her, but she handled it well and with a strong, yet sweet, spirit. She did not get mad at us and accuse us of making her look like a freak. She knew we loved her deeply because we have proven it to her every day for the past fifteen years. The storm came, and the relationship held strong.

If your child is going through a time of rebellion, it's tough on the whole family. I know.

Despite your best efforts to keep a strong relationship with your child, he may decide to try to overthrow the king and queen. This period of insurrection can strain relationships. One of our princesses went through a time of constantly challenging us, sneaking around, and exhibiting an overall terrible attitude. It affected all of us.

Tim Kimmel has some words of encouragement and wisdom to help us work with a child in such a situation: "Don't add bitterness to his rebellion. Keep all lines of communication open. Enjoy interaction with him outside the times you are forced to deal with his rebellious attitude. Give him plenty of reasons to believe you not only still love him, but also enjoy his company and have confidence in his future."[3]

If your child is going through a time of rebellion, it's tough on the whole family. I know. But your acts of love keep his heart attached to yours. Persevere with calmness. Make sure you're not adding to the volatility of the relationship with hurtful words, actions, or attitudes.

Rule Two: Keep Perspective

Since many of today's issues aren't directly addressed in Scripture (for example: entertainment choices, body piercing, teen drivers), we need to look for biblical principles with which to address various concerns. Key questions that can help get at the heart of an issue are "Where will this lead?" and "What is the child's motive or attitude?"

Jesus provides an example of using the first question when he speaks about false prophets: "Every good tree bears good fruit, but a bad tree bears bad fruit. A good tree cannot bear bad fruit, and a bad tree cannot bear good fruit" (Matthew 7:17, 18). Will the "fruit" of this situation lead to something good or bad? Will God be honored or not?

If I had asked this question ("Where will this lead?") when Princess One decided to wear one-dollar, secondhand shirts as her fashion statement, I could have easily answered, "Nowhere bad." (Maybe it would lead to her being more frugal and less fashion conscious. That would be good.) I would have realized that her motives were pure. She wasn't rebelling against our provision of new clothes. She was saying, "I'm original." However, my unreasonable expectations concerning the way I thought she should look destroyed my perspective, so I overreacted. I majored on a minor.

The opposite problem is minoring on majors—giving too little attention to important matters. It is crucial to keep perspective by asking "Where will this lead?" and "What is the child's motive or attitude?" Many times young moms minor on a major because they haven't answered the question "Where will this lead?" and they are ignorant of their child's motives or attitudes.

Eight-year-old Jill commanded her mom, "Mom, get my shoes for me."

"Honey, you go get your shoes."

"No! *You* get my shoes!"

Princess Jill has thrown down the gauntlet. What will this mom do? It would be faster for her to fetch the shoes and avoid a scene, but she must answer the question "Where will this lead?" Will Queen Mom reign or will Princess Jill? If Jill's mom can't see that giving in will put Jill on the throne and put *herself* in the position of a slave, she needs to answer the next question— "What is Jill's motive or attitude?" Is Princess Jill being lazy and demanding, or is she tired and stressed? Even if Jill is tired, she needs to talk to Queen Mom with respect, politely asking her to get the shoes.

After answering these questions, the queen has perspective to wisely deal with this situation and do what is best for her princess. She looks at the action in light of where it will lead and the attitude or motive behind the action.

Correctly answering these questions gives direction to maintaining a sense of proportion in your child's life. This is key as you deal with major issues and keep the minors minor. As a reforming control-freak mom, I am confessing to you that I used to major on everything. To me there were no minors. Everything was important and a potential slippery slope—clothes, jewelry, music, friends, free time, youth group . . . just everything. All of these things can be important, but how I handle them determines whether I make a minor issue an unnecessarily major deal.

 I am confessing to you that I used to major on everything. To me there were no minors.

I had the opportunity to practice maintaining a sense of proportion recently when Katie went for a hair appointment. All of our girls have beautiful red hair. Katie's hair is long and naturally curly. Or at least it *was*. Katie came home from her hair appointment and poked her head in the back door.

Ohmywordherhairisgone!

Katie's eyes met mine and asked, *Do you like my hair? Do I look OK?*

Keep smiling. You like this. You like this, I urged myself.

Katie's hair had gone from being a thick, curly mane cascading down the middle of her back to a layered cut of three-inch curls. (Picture this before you read on.)

Trying to keep my composure, I smiled as big as I could and said . . . Sorry, I can't remember what I said because I was in shock. But my words were positive. The most important thing here was not the loss of all Katie's gorgeous hair. The important thing was making sure she felt great about her new do. Her self-esteem and our relationship were more important than any amount of hair. The family complimented the new look, and life went on. Major issue averted.

One last word on hair. Joe White quotes an anonymous mom: "Who really cares if their hair is shaved funny or dyed a pretty color that you only see on rainbows? I'd rather have my kid come home with hair that makes me cringe than to rebel through the use of drugs. The rule I've had in our house is that I will pay for a standard haircut, but anything else comes out of their own pockets."[4]

Keeping a sense of proportion in every area of our kids' lives is accomplished only by having reasonable and biblical expectations. Paul warns us twice not to be unreasonable or harsh with our kids. He says, "Fathers, don't exasperate your children by coming down hard on them. Take them by the hand and lead them in the way of the Master" (Ephesians 6:4, *The Message*). He also says, "Fathers, don't aggravate your children. If you do, they will become discouraged and quit trying" (Colossians 3:21, *NLT*).

A young mom of a four-year-old confessed to our group, "I expected Nick to always be good. And then I thought, *I'm not always good. How can I expect him to always be good?*" While it is biblical for all of us to do our best to obey God, the truth is that we won't. How we respond to our kids' childish behavior or disobedience reflects whether we have majored on a minor or minored on a major.

 "Don't aggravate your children. If you do, they will become discouraged and quit trying."

God's actions are proportionate to the situation. For example, I struggle with my bad habit of nibbling on food throughout the day. I know this nibbling is why I battle to keep at a healthy weight. Yet God has not struck me with financial disaster or leprosy because I continue to give in to temptation. He gently deals with this shortcoming of mine by way of the scale creeping up, my clothes getting tighter, and convicting me. He is not shrugging off my "cute sin" and thinking, *Oh, Brenda will be Brenda. She has always had problems controlling her appetite.* No, there are consequences I must experience.

 ## We should major on what's important to God.

The wise Queen mom assesses a reasonable response to the situation.

If you're a laid-back mom, you may be smirking right about now at an uptight mom like me. Well, there is a word of caution here for you too. Having a more relaxed attitude does not guarantee that you are majoring on the majors. You may not have identified the majors, so you may be letting them slip by and mistakenly majoring on the minors, or nothing at all. We should major on what's important to God.

In Micah 6:8 God tells us, "He has showed you, O man, what is good. And what does the LORD require of you? To act justly and to love mercy and to walk humbly with your God." How do we act justly? The Ten Commandments are a good place to start. How do we love mercy and walk humbly with God? "Jesus replied, 'Love the Lord your God with all your heart and with all your soul and with all your mind.' This is the first and greatest commandment. And the second is like it: 'Love your neighbor as yourself'" (Matthew 22:37-39).

Mom, you need to know what the Bible says, and then you need to decide your majors and how they will define your kingdom.

So what's a major and what's a minor?

Major One: Character

God cares deeply about who we are. His Word is filled with instruction on what he desires us to be on the inside—that's character, and it's major. Respect, honesty, and purity are important aspects of character.

Respect

Respect is a huge nonnegotiable in our family. Kids need to respect God, their parents, authority, other people, and property. Here's what God says:

- Fear of the LORD is the beginning of knowledge. Only fools despise wisdom and discipline (Proverbs 1:7, *NLT*).
- Those who refuse to obey the laws of the land are refusing to obey God, and punishment will follow (Romans 13:2, *NLT*).
- Treat everyone you meet with dignity. Love your spiritual family. Revere God. Respect the government (1 Peter 2:17, *The Message*).
- Jesus went on to make these comments: If you're honest in small things, you'll be honest in big things; if you're a crook in small things, you'll be a crook in big things. If you're not honest in small jobs, who will put you in charge of the store? (Luke 16:10-12, *The Message*).
- Honor your father and mother. Then you will live a long, full life in the land the LORD your God will give you (Exodus 20:12, *NLT*).

A two-year-old can be just as disrespectful as a fifteen-year-old. That sassy attitude or swipe that came from your small child was an act of disrespect and defiance. Don't ignore it or rationalize it any longer. Deal with it now. You will have huge problems now and in the future if you don't. But if you do your job when your kids are young, you have a great chance of having a lot of fun with them when they are in elementary school, and the foundation for the teen years will be laid as well.

> Many times one of our princesses has received twice as much punishment as the other princess involved in the same crime because she rolled her eyes or used a sassy tone.

Respect is an ongoing battle with teens. They see disrespect all around them. Other kids aren't respectful, and sometimes those in authority over them aren't respectful to them. If we want respect from our kids, we must first give it to them. Then when they are disrespectful, deal with that before addressing whatever issue is on the table. Many times one of our princesses has received twice as much punishment as the other princess involved in the same crime because she rolled her eyes or used a sassy tone. She, of course, felt that was unfair. But I believe that disrespect poisons a life of promise. So I must emphasize the importance of being respectful.

Honesty

Honesty is a cousin to respect. A smooth operator can be convincingly respectful to the queen and yet be secretly planning a coup. Lying is on God's Top Seven list—one of the top seven things he hates. It is right up there with pride, murder, scheming evil, and stirring up trouble (Proverbs 6:16-19). The slightest infraction of dishonesty must be dealt with on a zero-tolerance level. There are no levels of honesty; either the person is telling the truth—all of it—or he is not.

Your child will catch this characteristic from the king and you. Are you honest in all areas? In my van there is a magazine I did not pay for. I accidentally picked it up from the waiting room at the car dealership. I've left it in the van so I can return it the next time I go to town. The kids have seen it every time they get in the van, and they know why it's there. Is the car dealer going to miss it? Of course not. But I know it's not mine, so it needs to be returned.

In being honest, I'm teaching honesty.

Purity

Purity is a condition of the mind and heart. If we want to stay pure and want the same for our kids, we need to put into action a plan to guard our minds (intellect) and hearts (emotions). David pledged to God, "I will set nothing wicked before my eyes" (Psalm 101:3, *NKJV*). Think about those words. Use them as a sieve for everything we will talk about in the next few paragraphs.

The attacks come from every angle in our society—the entertainment industry, fashion industry, media, and sometimes even from other parents. (What are we telling our kids by having coed sleepovers and chaperoned beer parties?) Purity is a tough area to maintain without locking our kids away or living a reclusive lifestyle. So let's proceed prayerfully, realizing that Jesus lived a perfect life while ministering to an imperfect society. Since our life's goal is to honor the Lord, sometimes we just have to say no. There is no way to rationalize much of what is out there.

My girls became teenagers and fashion conscious about the time that clothes became skintight, the shirts shrank up to the midriff, and the pants went down to . . . well, you get the picture.

 Jesus lived a perfect life while ministering to an imperfect society.

Shopping for clothes became WWIII. The princesses would bring armloads of "cute" clothes into the fitting room. Princess One would try on something, beaming with delight at how chic she looked. Princess Two would bump her out of the mirror to admire her own newfound look. They turned to get the queen's ruling.

"No way. They are too tight and too low. When you sit down I can see . . ."

"Mmmomm!! Quit that. It's sooooo cute. I can sit carefully and pull down my shirt."

"Sorry. No way."

Their disappointment turned to frustration then anger—directed, of course, at me and not at the fashion industry that so deserved it. In my girls' defense, there were not many options for teen girls. Either wear the latest trashy look, or dress like your mom (a fate worse than death).

I eventually came up with a system of measurements that we all agreed on. The shirts had to be a certain length from the shoulder to the hem. The back seam of the jeans also had to fit my code, and the shorts had to measure four of my fingers in length. If the item of clothing didn't "measure up," it was rejected. This standard kept arguments to a minimum, since many of the clothes didn't even make it to the dressing room.

The girls adjusted to the system and became creative in designing their own looks. I swallowed hard every time Katie wore gaudy, plaid, knit pants or her favorite look—a secondhand-store T-shirt, jean skirt with tube socks, and Chuck Taylor tennis shoes (none of the colors matched). I hated it, but she was covered appropriately and loved her unique look. That was important.

Joe White shares the wisdom of one mom: "Our rule was that as long as the clothing was not immodest, indecent, or vulgar, it was their choice. The clothes didn't have to match. . . . But the call on immodesty came down to Mom, not to them. They could wear ripped, ugly, smelly clothes if they wanted, but I found peer pressure was a great factor in them keeping their clothes clean."[5]

Clothes issues are one thing; the Internet is something else. The Internet presents a dangerous trap that can steal our kids' purity. People more knowledgeable than I have written books about the perils of the Internet, so I will keep my comments brief and personal. There are three main areas of concern regarding the Internet:

Easy access to pornography. A woman told me how shocked she was when she discovered her teen son and his friends had viewed porn on the Internet in her home—when she was there! She gave her son an appropriately severe consequence. Then she felt it was her responsibility to tell the other boys' mothers and apologize. Some would not believe their sons had participated. We are foolish parents if we don't acknowledge the dangerous connection between a teen boy's sex drive and the easy accessibility of porn, not to mention its addictiveness.

Instant Messaging (IM). Call this the gossip hotline. How easy it is for us to fall into a gossiping conversation when we are on the phone with a chatty friend for an extended period. Now think about our less mature kids in cyberspace using a screen name. They can say whatever they want about whomever they want . . . with no accountability. One of our dear princesses had her pure reputation smeared via IM by a girl who was jealous of her. Reports came to our daughter about what was being said, but not one "friend" stood up for her for fear this other girl would turn on them.

 The Internet presents a dangerous trap that can steal our kids' purity.

IM is also dangerous because emotional attachments are easily developed. I know of a nice Christian girl who has every creature comfort in her bedroom, including a computer. She stays up late IMing with a boy she knows from school and church, while her parents think she is doing homework. The more she and the boy talk, the more she falls for him. Yet, when he sees her at school, he is friendly, nothing more. Her heart is breaking, and he is clueless.

Chat rooms. The dangers are much the same as for IM but are increased because the kids are talking with complete strangers. We all know the deadly dangers of our kids bonding with these people, who may or may not be who they represent themselves to be.

We can do a few simple things to help our kids avoid unnecessary temptations and dangers. First, get the computers out of their bedrooms and into a room that has high visibility—

the kitchen, family room, or great room. I know the uproar will register on the Richter scale, but remember—you are the Queen Mom. When you rule, your kids benefit. It is highly unlikely they will get into stuff they shouldn't, when their computer activity is in plain sight.

Second, if you can't be home when the kids are, put a filter on the computer and set it high. Again, they will throw a fit, but if they aren't looking at what they shouldn't be, why should they care about the filter?

And finally, limit the time your child has on the computer for entertainment. Why does he need to spend all evening IMing with kids he just saw at school? When will there be time for family and for themselves? Dennis Rainey makes the point that your child has already spent at least eight hours at school with friends and teachers. He says, "Are you willing for him to spend one or two more hours on the phone every night with a boy friend or a girl friend? With homework, lessons, practices, and all, will you have any time with your teen to influence him?"[6]

 Would you let the dregs of society come in your front door and spend unlimited amounts of one-on-one time with your child?

Accountability is one tool parents are often too lazy or busy to pick up and use. With the computer, checking up is so easy. Every day or so, check the history to see where your child has been. Some kids are savvy enough to know how to erase the history. If that is the case, the previously discussed boundaries will give effective accountability. This accountability will also help your child stay away from temptations.

Would you let the dregs of society come in your front door and spend unlimited amounts of one-on-one time with your child? Of course not. We are doing just that when we take a hands-off attitude with the computer. As the queen you not only rule, you also protect your kingdom. Be strong. Set guidelines, and be there to enforce them. God's command to Joshua when Joshua took over the leading of Israel is appropriate for us: "Be strong and courageous Do not be terrified; do not be discouraged, for the LORD your God will be with you wherever you go" (Joshua 1:9).

What about movies and music? This is a real war zone for many families. You want to do all we have discussed to help your children make wise choices and have hearts after God; but sometimes they aren't there yet, so we need to take a stand.

I borrowed our movie rule from Susan Alexander Yates (author of ten books, international speaker on marriage and family, www.yatesbooks.com). Any movie other than a G-rated one must be approved. If one of our children is at a friend's house, she must first call home to get approval before she watches a particular movie. We have caught our kids in lies about this, and the consequences were appropriately severe, since they were both lying *and* being disobedient. (Remember, God is on your side. He wants them to get caught.)

When a request is made for a certain movie choice, find out for yourself what it's all about. My favorite Web site for getting the truth about what's in a movie is www.pluggedinonline.com. This site looks at a movie the way I would. It tells parents what we want and need to know. The subscription site www.screenit. com also gives an accurate evaluation of movies, including a description of potentially offensive scenes of violence, sexual content, drug use, etc. This site even gives the number of times each swear word is used.

After review, discuss with the fledgling royal why he wants to see this particular movie. Ask him if he would be willing to ask the Lord for his guidance. Pray with your child, and give the Holy Spirit time to work in him. If your prince comes to you with a straight face and tells you that the Lord said he could watch an R-rated movie you disapprove of, you will need to smack him over the head with your scepter! No, not really, but you will need to rule that this R-rated movie is not acceptable and watching it will result in serious consequences. (Note that some PG-13 movies are worse than some R-rated ones.)

> If your prince comes to you with a straight face and tells you that the Lord said he could watch an R-rated movie you disapprove of, you will need to smack him over the head with your scepter!

Music is even harder for me to make a judgment about because I can't understand most of the words. But music can be more influential than movies because the words get stuck in our kids' minds; they sing the lyrics over and over without even thinking.

The previously mentioned www.pluggedinonline.com is a great place to find out exactly what's in a song. The Web site www.CPYU.org is also a priceless tool for parents to find out what's up in current music and culture. But moms, be ready when you visit this site. It goes to today's culture and deals with the stuff I do my best to keep out of my home and mind. CPYU (Center for Parent/Youth Understanding) does a great job of presenting the latest and helping us parents find the good and bad in it. These two sites give parents the reality of what's in their kids' entertainment choices. However, you may need to get the song lyrics printed out to present to your defiant royal. You can find these at www.lyrics-songs.com. Have him read the disgusting and vulgar words aloud to you. This may be just the reality jolt he needs so he can make better music choices.

> Why do so many of us stay silent when our kids come up with half-baked, silly, or just plain stupid plans?

Again, if he chooses to throw down the gauntlet on this issue, be ready for battle. We did not allow the kids to buy music we believed to be inappropriate. We also didn't allow inappropriate CDs that their friends burned for them. If they buy forbidden CDs, feel free to take them and destroy them (if they can't be returned). If your prince chooses to break a rule when he purchases a CD, he also loses the fifteen dollars he spent on the CD. If the CD comes from a friend, it gets returned to that friend. I'm not naive enough to believe I can keep my kids from hearing the junk that their friends are listening to, but I can do what I can do. That is all I'm responsible for.

Take your choices to the Lord and see what he has to say. Ultimately, the heavenly Father is the only one you will answer to about how you parented your kids.

Major Two: Personal Safety

Personal safety is definitely a major. We parents cannot ignore our responsibility to keep our kids safe. Why then do so many of us stay silent when our kids come up with half-baked, silly, or just plain stupid plans? And why do we let them walk out the door when we don't know their plans? We are devastated when we hear that a child or teen has been injured or killed in an accident. My heart breaks for those families. Yet many times I ask, "What were they doing out at that time of night?" or "Why were they doing this activity in the first place?" or (most often) "Where were the parents to supervise this activity or say no?"

I know these are unpopular and hard questions. And accidents do happen. But there are things we can do to prevent the opportunity for many accidents.

The Need for Supervision

All kids need to be supervised, in varying degrees, depending on their ages.

Regarding infants, if you need to leave the room, always leave the baby in a safe, confined place such as a crib or playpen and out of reach of small children and animals. Consider using an audio and/or visual monitor. Keep your radar turned on with toddlers. Always know what they are up to and where they are. If it gets quiet, look out. Toddlers are safest with you and not playing in another room. Preschoolers can play on their own, but again, keep the radar on and check on them frequently.

When kids move into the junior high years, many moms are too eager to pass them off as adults.

Elementary-school children can play on their own, but check on them frequently to see how they are using their imaginations. They should not be left at home alone. Even if they are trustworthy, they are not mature enough to handle an emergency. Remember, you are the mom, and your kids are top priority.

When kids move into the junior high years, many moms are too eager to pass them off as adults. Junior highers are allowed to babysit kids of all ages for long periods of time. They are allowed to stay home unsupervised. This is an age when kids may think they are mature enough to try adult things, such as alcohol and sex. I would strongly urge you to be home or make arrangements for a trusted adult to be home with your junior high kids when you can't be. This can be a make-it-or-break-it time.

One of my daughters listened in shock as one of the most popular girls in high school shared how she began drinking in eighth grade with older kids. This grew into a habit. Thankfully, friends prayed for her, and God got her attention when she was sixteen. She is living for him and no longer drinking. But had there been parental supervision, this girl could have been saved years of misery.

Another mom once told me, "I always know my daughter is safe when she is with you." I wonder how she feels the rest of the time.

Junior high kids also think they are old enough to hang out at the mall unchaperoned. You gotta be kidding! There are sick people out there just looking for a fresh-faced, innocent girl or boy. They go where the kids are. Much to our daughters' chagrin, I have accompanied them on trips to the mall with friends. I have coffee in the general vicinity where the girls are shopping. I stay as far from them as I can, and yet I'm able to see the entrance to the store. Of course, they must stay together at all times. Another mom once told me, "I always know my daughter is safe when she is with you." I wonder how she feels the rest of the time.

This is a good time to start introducing your teens to some

of the harsh truths of life. They need to know the world is not a safe place and that your boundaries for them are to keep them safe while they have fun.

The high-school years can be a real challenge. Older teens' boundaries need to be extended but not removed, so use common sense when giving permission for your teens' plans. Make sure you have the answers to these questions before you say yes:

- 👑 Does this sound like a safe activity?
- 👑 Will the parents be home?
- 👑 Do I know the parents?
- 👑 Do they share my values? Are they responsible?
- 👑 Who will be going?
- 👑 Do I know the other kids?
- 👑 What kind of kids are they, and how do my kids behave in their presence?

The Need for Communication

Another nonnegotiable for our kids is that they must call home if plans change—location, kids in attendance (reasonably, within their ability to judge the other kids' influence on the group), or major change in activity (an evening at the movies turned into a poker game at Matt's house).

Let your teen know that he can call you (and you, him, since he is carrying a cell phone) at any time for any reason. If he does call and is looking for an exit, it's very important that you don't go ballistic on him. He is reaching out to you—don't make him sorry. If he calls after he's already participated in questionable, destructive, immoral, or illegal behavior, pick him up with love that registers on your face and in your heart. Then when everyone has cooled down, deal with the situation in a reasonable way. Most importantly, you must be available to get the call!

· ·

If you understand that—and the other points in this chapter—I crown you One Cool Queen Mom!

Royal Decree

Reigning as Queen Mom is a process. It starts with a mind-set that leads us to discover God's plan for our families. As we discern God's majors and minors, we'll see a positive effect on our daily decisions. And that is how we reign—day by day, doing what God has shown us to do. What is he calling you to do this week? Do it!

Royal Inquiry

1. Why is a sense of proportion important in your mothering?

2. How can you overcome some of the obstacles to developing a strong relationship with your child?

3. Have you ever thought about the questions "Where will this lead?" and "What is the child's motive or attitude?" Will you make a point to do so the next time your child throws a fit? tells you what to do? uses a sassy tone? tells (not asks) you what he is going to do?

4. Which sections dealing with your child's character present the biggest struggle for you? What are practical things you can do this week to make progress?

5. Is there a major that you have been minoring in? Is there a minor that you have been majoring in? What are you going to do about it?

chapter ten

Future Kingdoms in Distant Lands

Preparing and Releasing Our Kids for the Rest of Their Lives

Time passed, and the kingdom flourished under the king and queen's reign. The years had gone so quickly, it hardly seemed possible that the prince would soon turn thirteen. The kingdom made preparations for the spectacular celebration.

The special evening climaxed when the king and queen bestowed a crown on the prince. "You are almost a man, son," they proclaimed. "This crown symbolizes the new responsibilities and privileges you will now have in this exciting time of your life."

Good for the king and queen! They realize the prince needs to be released to become a man and that this involves new responsibilities and privileges. However, because the king and queen have failed to train him, he is unprepared for this stage of release.

I remember holding each of my babies, only a few hours old, and soaking in the wonder of this new person. I was gripped by intense love for her, even though I had met her only moments ago. I was willing to sacrifice and surrender my life, if necessary, to give her the best life I could. Any thought of this infant becoming her own person, growing up, and leaving me didn't exist in the midst of my maternal exhilaration and the soon-to-follow daily survival tasks of feeding, bathing, diapering, doing laundry, feeding again . . . and again.

We should do our job so well that we are no longer needed. So much for job security.

The sad and ironic part of a mom's job is that when we are really good moms, giving our best—time, talents, love, patience, wisdom, and energy—we feel deeply the pain that comes when the recipients of all our gifts leave us for their own adventures.

We should do our job so well that we are no longer needed. So much for job security, but being Queen Mom is a temporary job. Oh yes, we will always be our children's moms, yet we will not always be Queen Mom. Our job is to prepare each child toward being independent in this world. To release the child all along, in age-appropriate ways, will make the last release a smooth segue from the adult-to-child relationship into an adult-to-adult relationship.

Preparing

Ultimately, our job is not only to raise our kids to be mature and responsible but also to help them discover who God made them uniquely to be.

Your prince may be a mirror image of the king, or he may have a personality like none other. The other day I was talking with a father of two sons who were opposite in every way. This man was athletic in his youth and still loves sports. One son is just like his dad—in appearance, interests, and talents. The other son is nothing like his dad. As we talked, this father's struggle to accept the latter son was clear. I know this man loves both sons, but he couldn't quite figure out how to accept and appreciate the son who was so different from him.

This story is not unusual. God has given most parents at least one child who is a puzzle to them. I smile when I think of some of my outgoing friends with not-so-outgoing sons. The parents want the boys to be social, but the boys would rather play a video game. I can chuckle because I married one of those not-so-outgoing guys. He turned out to be a great husband and dad; he just doesn't care to be the life of the party.

We need to accept our children and do our best to understand, support, and help them become the persons God designed them to be.

Examples of parent and child mismatches are endless. Parents with exceptional IQs strain to identify with a child who struggles in school. Parents with average IQs feel inferior to their genius child. Parents gifted athletically can't understand why their athletically gifted child wants to pursue his art talent. Parents who are not dreamers can't understand the dreams and aspirations of their prodigy. Not understanding and accepting our children can cause division in our relationships with them. Ralph Woerner, a retired pastor and author, writes, "When parents try to force them into a mold which doesn't fit their temperament or personality . . . they become bitter."[1]

We need to accept our children and do our best to understand, support, and help them become the persons God designed them to be. Three key elements help us know and understand a person: personality, interests, and talents. When we have figured out these individual pieces, the puzzle of who our child is comes together.

Know Your Child's Personality

Some great books have been written about personalities, and I won't attempt to cover material they already have.[2] But here's a brief summary of four different personality types to get you thinking about the makeup of your children.

- *Sanguine*—also referred to as an otter. Outgoing, loves people, is enthusiastic, expressive.
- *Choleric*—compared to a lion. Also outgoing, but as a strong leader. Strong-willed, decisive, organizes well.
- *Melancholy*—compares well to a beaver. Likes to be alone. Deep thinker, analytical, creative, detail oriented.
- *Phlegmatic*—also called a golden retriever. Laid-back and easygoing. Patient, peacemaker, good listener.

Are you saying "Aha!" as you start to solve the mystery of who your prince or princess is? Do you understand why your child is forever being corrected for talking in class? tries to tell you and the king how to raise the other children? prefers working on his music to having friends over? seems to be a better friend to her friends than they are to her . . . and that doesn't bother her?

Personality is one part of how your child is wired—the way God made him. Our personalities will never change. But we need to let the Holy Spirit work on our weaknesses so we become more like Jesus. The wise mom understands the extent to which the child's personality plays out in his life.

One thing that attracted me to my husband was his focus on me. He seemed captivated by me. He didn't need to work the room or be the life of the party. I loved this (and I still do); however, I used to get frustrated when he didn't mingle in social situations. He was content to sit and watch others. I thought he looked lonely, but he wasn't. He was happy. I was the one who wanted him to circulate and make small talk. That is so *not* Gene. Now that I've accepted what I know about Gene—that he is not the social butterfly that I am—we are both happy at social events. He talks to one person at a time or just sits and relaxes while I get my social fix talking to almost every person in the room.

Are you expecting things from your child that he or she can never do?

What do you know about your child's personality? Now, with that in mind, truthfully admit your expectations for your child's behavior. Do the two go together? Are you expecting things from your child that he or she can never do? Begin to accept and embrace the personalities of each of your children, no matter how different those personalities are from your own.

Know Your Child's Interests

Interests stir our curiosity. Interests make us want to learn more. God gave each of us interests as part of who we are. Interests reveal themselves as cravings, impulses, longings, passions . . . some yearning to be satisfied. Until we explore the urgings we get from our interests, we will be incomplete in who God made us to be. When our kids are given the opportunity to discover what interests them, they gain greater depth in understanding who they are.

My grandma once shared with me a secret piece of the puzzle of who she is. She was a teenager in Missouri during the Great Depression, and her parents were farmers. My grandma's life was good but definitely not glamorous. She worked hard, but she also had a spirit of beauty and sophistication. When she was about twenty, she let that spirit carry her on a train to the faraway land of Nebraska. She sold her horse for money for the train ticket, and she sold her cow (her dowry) for tuition money so she could realize her dream of going to cosmetology school. She did well and graduated. She came home with her degree and enthusiasm, but opportunities for a new beautician were not available in her small farming community. Besides, the handsome, nice farm boy from down the road was coming around a lot. Before long she was married, and soon a baby was on the way.

Is your child too busy to explore what excites him? Discovering the interests God put in us takes time. Too many commitments eat up the time needed for thinking, exploring, and discovering.

My grandma doesn't regret her life decisions, but when she talked about this adventure, her voice had a tone of enthusiasm and confidence that I had not heard before. This spirit of adventure for pursuing dreams is still alive in her.

What makes your child's face shine with excitement? What keeps your son talking or reading or discovering? What does your daughter pursue with endless enthusiasm?

Princess Two did a brave thing by stepping out of marching band her senior year. Being in the fall play had given her a taste for the stage, and her interest in dance team was rekindled by her friends who were on the team. Many of her band peers didn't understand. After all, how did she know for *sure* she would make the play and dance team tryouts? But our princess was willing to take the chance because she knew this would be her last opportunity for these activities. To support her in this decision, I went with her when she told the band directors she was choosing not to be in marching band. Senior year may have been her last chance to fulfill her longing to be a Rockette. I didn't want her to miss it.

Is your child too busy to explore what excites him? Discovering the interests God put in us takes time. Too many commitments eat up the time needed for thinking, exploring, and discovering.

Know Your Child's Talents

God has given each of us talents. Talents are abilities that seem to come naturally to us and then need to be developed. My family and I love watching the winter Olympics. All the athletes who make it to the Olympics are dedicated and hardworking. However, a few athletes outshine their peers. They seem to have that extra something that no amount of hard work or dedication can bring. They are naturally and exceptionally gifted in their sports.

As we watch the Olympics, we also notice that the athletes' parents are the ones yelling the loudest from the stands. They wave their countries' flags and hold signs. They cry for their Olympians' victories and defeats. I wonder where these Olympians would be if their parents had ignored their children's talents and insisted they pursue an area of the parents' interest or expertise.

Best-selling author and international speaker Florence Littauer tells the story of her mother-in-law in her last years, when a nurse cared for her at home. She had declined to the point that she did not recognize anyone or communicate with anyone. During one of Florence's visits, the nurse told her that her mother-in-law stood up after dinner and sang beautifully. Florence reflected how her mother-in-law always wanted to be an opera singer, but *her* mother did not allow her to explore this talent. Florence ended with, "Mother died with the music still in her."[3]

I don't want my child to die "with the music still in her." I want her to realize and enjoy being the person God made her to be.

After some thought, reflection, and analysis, what have you discovered about your child? Is he the person you thought he was, or did you get a glimpse of someone you don't recognize?

In the movie *A Cinderella Story*, Sam, the Cinderella character (played by Hilary Duff), has a secret relationship with her mystery prince, Austin, through the technology of instant messaging. In their correspondence, Austin tells Sam that his dad has a plan for him that is not at all what he wants. His dad wants him to go to his alma mater and play football. Austin is the high school's football hero, but he wants to attend Princeton and become a poet. Austin tries to talk to his dad about his dreams, but his dad won't hear him. Finally, at the end of the movie, Austin has had enough. Austin runs off the football field during the big game.

"What are you doing?" his father asks.

"I'm outta here."

"You're throwing away your dream!"

"No, Dad, I'm throwing away *yours*."

Will you help your prince discover and become who God wired him to be? He may have to drop athletics so he can pursue his music. Even though your son is talented in football, God may be calling him to be a praise and worship leader, and he will need training in music and serious time with the Lord to be prepared.

Is your child consumed with activities you've piled on his plate—to the extent that he doesn't have the opportunity to experiment in the areas of interest God gave him? Some of my daughters' friends complain that they must stay in a certain activity because their parents make them. The girls say they are tired of the activity but won't tell their moms because they would be angry—the moms expect the girls to excel in these areas. I know kids whine to each other and don't always mean what they say, but my concern is that the girls feel they can't tell their moms. They may be using their moms as an excuse, or they may truly not feel free to talk with them. We need to hold these activities loosely, so our kids are free to talk to us about how they really feel.

 Will you help your prince discover and become who God wired him to be?

Last summer, Princess Three surprised us with her announcement that she wanted to join the swim team. Where did this interest come from? She loves to swim, but competitively? I discussed with her the time and work involved. She understood and still wanted to be on the team. So I signed her up and bought the suit, goggles, team flannel pants and sweatshirt (with her name on it). She was set. She went to a week of practice. She wasn't great, but she kept trying. On the day of her first swim meet, I raced home from a two-day writing conference just in time to see her compete. She looked so cute in her swimsuit and goggles. She gave each event her best effort. The next day she confided in me her desire to quit the team.

"Are you sure?" I asked. "You will get better with practice."

"I just don't want to do it anymore."

After more gentle conversation and some prying, the reason surfaced: "I like to swim. I just don't like to compete."

We got to the real reason. Competition is not her thing. Some kids love it, but not Kerry. Since the coach had a two-week tryout policy, and we were still in the first week, Kerry was able to graciously withdraw. I could almost see the load lift from her shoulders when we made that decision. Her perky personality was back.

 "God causes all things to work together for good to those who love God."

I know many parents have a never-quit policy. We don't believe in letting our kids quit, thereby not fulfilling their commitments. But Princess Three was still in the tryout time frame. Her leaving the team did not create a hole, because the roster had not yet been made. We finish what we start, but when we see something isn't working, we know we can make changes before a new commitment is made. This policy teaches kids responsibility, and it gives them room to explore other interests.

When you deal with each particular situation, ask yourself, *How can I best handle the current situation to better prepare my child for release?* Everything we do in our mothering is to prepare our children to be able to thrive on their own. So for all the miscellaneous life situations, let that question be your guide.

God parents us this way. He is alert to every detail of our lives. The Bible tells us that "even the very hairs of your head are all numbered" (Matthew 10:30).

As Queen Moms, we need to be attentive to using each situation in our kids' lives to better prepare them for future release.

God is keeping track of every hair in my daughters' thick manes as well as every hair that falls from my husband's handsome head! If God cares that much about our hair, he is not going to let any detail of our lives slip by. He is alert to everything and uses every opportunity to get us where he wants us to be. "We know that God causes all things to work together for good to those who love God, to those who are called according to His purpose. For whom He foreknew, He also predestined to become conformed to the image of His Son" (Romans 8:28, 29, *NASB*).

God's goal is to conform us to the image of Jesus. He doesn't slack off or let up. "There has never been the slightest doubt in my mind that the God who started this great work in you would keep at it and bring it to a flourishing finish on the very day Christ Jesus appears" (Philippians 1:6, *The Message*). God knows how to best use each situation in our lives to prepare us for the day of Christ's return. As Queen Moms, we need to be attentive to using each situation in our kids' lives to better prepare them for future release.

Releasing

The Queen Mom must ensure that every situation her child goes into is *safe*. I say that with all that is in me. Don't back down. If your Queen Mom red flag goes up, pay attention to it. I don't care where you are or whom you are with—take your child and leave that situation. Does a day go by when the news programs don't report on a child being victimized? We are our children's protectors. Our kids trust us to keep them safe. We can't let them down.

I cannot allow my children to do the things my cautious mom allowed me to do when I was a child. My sisters and I walked to school—and home for lunch every day. We played deep in the woods for lengthy chunks of time. We rode our bikes within a few blocks' perimeter in our neighborhood. I hate the fact that I cannot allow my girls the privilege of these ceremonial releasings, but today's society has given me no choice.

I am the mom who makes the phone calls to research and ensure that appropriate safety boundaries are in place so I can release the girls to participate in their fun activities.

> **If Jesus prayed for us not to be led into temptation, why should we lead our kids there?**

Princess Two wanted to go on a mission trip with a parachurch organization. I talked about safety issues with the man in charge of the trip. At the end of our conversation, I knew that we did not have the same definition of safety.

I realize my girls will never be totally safe, and I release them into situations knowing that something may happen. But I want to know that the adults involved are knowledgeable about my child's location and situation. In my opinion, the kids going on the mission trip were not prepared for the questionable elements they would (and did) encounter as a result of loose security. Many parents felt this would be a good experience for their teens. Since I couldn't agree with the safety guidelines for this trip, we decided this would not be a good experience for our daughter. I am not saying other parents made a wrong choice. I am saying this was not the choice for us. (I am glad to report that everyone came home safely from the trip.)

Asking appropriate questions can keep our kids from harm. Recently, two teenage boys from our high school were involved in a serious car accident. They were at a party at another boy's home, and alcohol was served. A couple of major alarms go off in me about this situation. Why did the parents of the kids attending the party not check the details? *Where are you going? Will the parents be home and actively chaperoning? Do I know the parents?* A negative answer to any of these questions immediately shuts down the plans. If I don't know and trust the parents or if I can't get a solid recommendation from another parent I trust . . . then no way.

We need to learn to trust our kids, but we also need to make sure they are not being tempted past what they can handle. Why allow our kids to go into situations where we know they will be tempted? Jesus prayed: "Lead us not into temptation, but deliver us from the evil one" (Matthew 6:13). If Jesus prayed for us not to be led into temptation, why should we lead our kids there? Jesus also told the inner circle of disciples, "Watch and pray so that you will not fall into temptation. The spirit is willing, but the body is weak" (Matthew 26:41).

When Potiphar's wife tried to seduce Joseph, "he refused to go to bed with her or even be with her" (Genesis 39:10). Then one day she made her final move on him, but "he left his cloak in her hand and ran out of the house" (v. 12). Joseph knew that in order to stay obedient to God, he had to get out of the tempting situation. God is serious about our protecting ourselves from temptation, so why shouldn't we protect our kids from dangerous—and avoidable—temptations?

I also pay attention to my child's red flags. If she says someone is creepy or makes her feel weird, I listen! God gave our children gut feelings too. The fact that we are listening and acknowledging these feelings helps our children become confident and discerning.

Releasing Your Baby

The wise Queen Mom realizes at the birth of her baby that she needs to be working toward the day of total release, when her baby becomes an adult. The Queen Mom knows that her time of influencing and teaching the child is short compared with the totality of the child's life. She must use her opportunities well and not try to hang on when the time for release comes.

Even when the child is an infant, the wise Queen Mom resists the urge to pick up the baby every time she whimpers. Yes, she needs to be checked on, but a baby princess also needs to learn to put herself back to sleep and to entertain herself.

My mom had five princesses in seven years. (I hurt just thinking about it!) One of my sisters and I were in school the fall my youngest sister was born. Mom had a seven- and a six-year-old to get ready for school, while a four- and a two-year-old ran around the house and an infant cried in her crib. Mom recalls, "I had to let Karen cry for a bit while I got you and Debbie ready for school. I had the rest of the day to take care of her."

You know what? Karen turned out to be the most easygoing and merciful of all five of us girls. Those few minutes of crying didn't hurt Karen, and Mom appropriately released her so she could mature a little and not grow into a spoiled child.

Do you see my mom's confident releasing of Karen? Mom knew what she needed to do—get two daughters ready for school. She knew that picking up the baby every time she cried would lead to more crying and more dependence on her, which is exactly what she didn't want. Our goal is to help our children become less dependent on us.

> **A patronizing wife can quickly demean her husband, thereby taking away his desire to assert himself in this new adventure of being King Dad.**

Another major level of release is leaving the baby with someone else. I have talked with many young moms who don't trust their husbands with their children. I wonder why they married a man they can't trust. Would the new King Dad benefit from a primer on child care? Do this in a way that isn't condescending. Do you remember when you learned to drive? Was the person who taught you kind and patient, or did he jump on every mistake you made? If he did the latter, no doubt you felt angry, nervous, and insecure. You were likely to make more mistakes because he rattled your confidence. A patronizing wife can quickly demean her husband, thereby taking away his desire to assert himself in this new adventure of being King Dad. Help the king learn the skills he needs for his new role; then trust him.

We also often struggle with leaving the baby with someone other than the king. Again, safety must be the prime concern. I question the wisdom of leaving infants in the care of teen girls. So many unexpected situations can arise with a newborn that even the most responsible teen girl does not have the knowledge or maturity to handle. Now that I have two teen daughters, I am even more tenacious in my belief. Suppose one of my girls were babysitting an infant when something happened that she couldn't handle or prevent, and the baby was hurt . . . or worse. Not only would the family of the infant suffer, my daughter would bear that scar for the rest of her life. I know that finding a babysitter college age or older is harder, but it is definitely worth the trouble.

Princess One is a sensitive personality, and her sensitivity was evident even as a baby. The crying began with the tiniest variance in her comfort. She was not easily soothed. When she was about four weeks old, we left her with my mother-in-law. About an hour and a half into our date, we called home to see how Katie was doing. My sister-in-law answered the phone. Katie had been crying since we left, so my mother-in-law had called my sister-in-law to come help with this screaming, redheaded tyrant. We felt awful for my mother-in-law. We didn't leave Katie with her again until Katie was a toddler.

Another time we had to leave Katie with one of my mom's best friends while our family went to my grandmother's funeral. Again, Katie was not happy with this arrangement, so she cried most of the time. This woman was not bothered by Katie's unhappiness. She did everything she could for Katie, and then she laid her on a blanket on the floor and let her cry—all the while sitting next to her. It broke my heart to learn that Katie had been unhappy for so long, but we needed to be at the funeral. Katie was not hurt. She was in the best of hands; Mom's friend was a trusted, mature, experienced woman. We had to release Katie.

I'm not saying you should leave your screaming kids no matter what. Do everything you can to make this separation not be traumatic, using a security blanket, toys, or a pacifier. Then go. Dr. James Dobson assures parents that this short time of separation is good for parent and child and will not harm the child: "Generally speaking, you are not going to hurt your child emotionally by doing what you need to do, and then coming back to get him."[4]

As your child progresses into the preschool years, look for opportunities to release her. Let her play at a friend's house while you grocery shop. Allow her to dress herself or get a juice box from the fridge. Give her freedom to do art projects her way. One of my favorite Christmas tree ornaments is a paper angel that Princess Three made in preschool. The angel's only decoration is a scribble of black crayon across its middle. Every year we all laugh when we are reminded of Kerry's "black period" in her artwork.

Each of these release opportunities allows your child to separate from you as she becomes her own person. She learns she can do well without you. Each similar occasion becomes a vital building block in her preparation for complete release.

In truth, we are releasing our kids to the care of God. We are saying to God that we have done everything he asks of us as moms and that we trust him with the outcome.

Releasing Your Elementary-Age Child

Ah, then come the school years. The first day of school separates the introverts from the extroverts. My girls climbed into the bus and hardly looked back. After the bus drove down the street, I let my shoulders drop and the tears flow. It wasn't easy letting go of them for the day, but I knew it was best for them.

My heart goes out to the mom whose child is crying as his mom drops him at his classroom. She must deal with his heartbreak and her own. If a child does not adjust well to a classroom setting, many factors must be explored. Maybe the child is not ready for a classroom. Is the teacher's personality making the child feel intimidated or insecure? After a careful, fact-finding investigation, make a decision. But please make sure the decision is best for your child. Don't decide to homeschool a child because you can't stand to see him put in a situation where he will be challenged to grow and mature.

 Our kids are not our security blankets, and we must let them go.

Remember, parenting is not about us. It's about doing what is best for our kids. If you can't separate your emotions from the situation, talk with a trusted friend or pastor who knows you and your child. Our kids are not our security blankets, and we must let them go.

I had to go on a fact-finding investigation the first week Princess One entered first grade. Princess One had done great in half-day kindergarten; however, her first week of first grade was a nightmare. She came home from school in a fury and threw herself onto the couch, sobbing uncontrollably. Since she was eager to go to school in the morning, I was clueless about what was going on. I made an appointment with her teacher. She saw no evidence of Katie's struggling in class, but her years of mothering and teaching experience gave her wisdom about Katie's difficulties. Katie was the youngest in her class, and at age six, the difference in her level of maturity compared to the older kids was evident. The teacher felt that Katie struggled to handle the stress of a full day at school because of her age difference.

What should we do? Put her back in kindergarten? The teacher said Katie was too bright to go back. Homeschool? Maybe, but the teacher shared that her own daughter had been through the same situation when she was a first-grader. The teacher wanted to keep Katie in her class and work with me to help her through this transition. So we did. After about two weeks, Katie was back in her stride and loving school. She has been an excellent student ever since. Wise moms gather facts and wise counsel before they make a major decision about what is best for their kids.

School brings on many opportunities to prepare our kids for the real world. Let kids handle these challenges, thereby getting them closer to their total release. Our kids will have battles with other students and teachers. I equip mine to handle what they can at their own level. Then if that fails, I decide whether it is an issue worth pursuing. Since life is unfair and we can't make every situation be the best for our child's benefit, we must decide whether what's at stake is worth the fight. Sometimes the most valuable life lessons are learned when we help our kids handle an unfair situation graciously.

 Our kids will have battles with other students and teachers. I equip mine to handle what they can at their own level.

If I decide to pursue a particular issue, the next step is for me to get involved as my child's protector in order to keep the conflict fair. I contact the authority directly involved with the situation, calmly and respectfully explain the problem, and ask for his or her help in resolving it. I am not demanding or bossy, but simply asking for help. I have not needed to do this often, and have had only a couple of times when I didn't get help, requiring me to contact the next level of authority. Then the situation usually was resolved.

Let me tell you about two situations with two different outcomes.

Princess Three's fifth-grade year was extremely hard on her. A number of difficult circumstances befell her class that year. The class had several disruptive boys. When they got going, many of the other boys, who normally were well behaved, joined in the revelry. The teacher was a delightful, young woman, but her inexperience was no match for these boys. The principal, who was always alert and attentive to each child and teacher, had severe health problems that kept him out of school much of the year. If he had been at school, he would have dealt swiftly with the poor behavior. So these boys wreaked havoc in class with few repercussions. As a result, Princess Three was stressed and anxious.

I talked with the teacher, and she assured me she had the situation under control. Nothing changed. I talked with the principal. He apologized for not being available to help the teacher and said they would work on a plan. Nothing changed. Kerry's anxiety caused her to have migraine headaches. We prayed together, and our family gave her comfort and encouragement in every way we could.

Kerry got through the year, learning valuable life lessons. She learned that everyone isn't always well behaved, and she learned how to cope in difficult circumstances. She learned that sometimes we have to bear with the unfair situation. She also saw the mistakes her teacher made and gained great insight into what works and doesn't work in disciplining kids. I hated seeing her go through this situation. But since she endured and learned from it, the result is that she is becoming a poised, mature young lady.

Our next situation had a better immediate outcome. In one of our princess's classes, a number of boys (sorry, I'm not trying to pick on the boys!) were saying inappropriate things to her and justifying it by insisting they were only teasing. In the business world this behavior would be considered sexual harassment. We explained to our daughter the need to tell these boys flat out not to talk that way *around* her or *to* her. She did so, but they persisted. I made an appointment with the teacher, and my daughter and I met with him. He realized the seriousness of the situation, and immediately the three of us went to meet with the principal. The next day the principal dealt with the boys in a way they understood.

Do you see the progression for resolution?

1. Our princess told us about the problem. We told her how to communicate clearly to the boys to stop.
2. She did as we instructed her.
3. After no results I stepped in and calmly communicated with the appropriate level of authority.
4. This gave the teacher room to do the right thing, which was to go to the principal.
5. The principal did his job—protecting our princess and getting these boys straightened out.

Not only did the harassment stop, after the boys had their "talk" with the principal, they treated our princess with kindness and respect. I realize this type of scenario could have a number of contributing factors that might have made the situation urgent. If that were the case, I would have gone straight to the teacher and principal before allowing my daughter back in the class. I did what Gene and I felt was appropriate for the situation.

What if your child is having conflict with a teacher or another child because of your child's own poor behavior? When a conflict arises, get the facts. We don't always know *everything* about our children. Be ready to hear the hard truth about your prince or princess. It will be to your child's benefit to deal with it now.

> Letting children face the real-life consequences of their poor behavior prepares them for life and is a step toward our releasing them.

If, after your exploration into the situation, you discover your child is at fault, let him suffer whatever consequences come with the offense. Do not rescue him or coddle him; if you do, it will cripple him—and in his eyes, your authority with him is weakened. He needs to learn these lessons while he is young and at home so he won't have to learn them the hard way in the real world.

If someone approaches you to tattle on your child, be cool. Just listen. Don't acknowledge that the accusation is right or wrong. Let the person know you will check it out and get back to her. Be prepared, though, because most likely she will be coming to you with a major attitude and will want you to admit your child is wrong and that you will punish him for the next decade. There are often two sides to a story. I check with trusted, unbiased sources before I question one of my girls. I am always ready to admit that my daughter was wrong if she indeed was wrong. (But if she wasn't wrong, I will not say she was.) Letting children face the real-life consequences of their poor behavior prepares them for life and is a step toward our releasing them. We are on our way to raising mature adults.

Releasing Your Teen

With our boundaries and rules in place, Gene and I can, much of the time, let consequences do the teaching. Teens learn to make good decisions when they must face the consequences of their decisions. This is a beneficial teaching tool, because at this time in teens' lives, the consequences of these decisions are less likely to be life-changing than if they learned them in the not-so-forgiving adult world.

For instance, we gave Princess Two a curfew of midnight for a Saturday night party. She had the choice to stay out till midnight or come home earlier. Remember, our rule is that the family goes to Sunday school and church. Our social butterfly chose to stay out until 11:45 PM (making sure I knew she was home fifteen minutes early). She accepted the consequence of being tired for church and having to drag herself out of bed to be ready to leave with us on time Sunday morning.

The allowance we give our girls is not all free money. This money has purposes, such as savings, gifts, tithing, and spending for their activities and wants. Princess Two presented me with the order form for the high-school yearbook. I told her I would pay half. She has the means to save for the other half if she really wants the yearbook. I haven't heard about it again. Different families can work these things out differently. The point is not to match *my* plan, but to *have* a plan.

I am preparing the girls for adulthood and releasing them by not making life unrealistically easy for them. Princess Two did not make a bad decision to stay out till her curfew, but she did have to endure the consequences: hauling herself out of bed early Sunday morning. Having a high-school yearbook is fine, but not a necessity. We have amply provided our princess the means to have one, if she chooses to spend her money that way. Adulthood is full of decisions, sacrifices, and consequences. Our job is to help the kids learn to deal with these issues before they leave home.

Our oldest princess is a sophomore in college. Many of her friends are "living on their own." Actually, they're not really on their own, because even though they're in apartments (not dorms), their parents are paying all their living expenses, their credit card bills, and providing spending money. At what point in their children's lives will the parents release them and let them stand alone? The sad thing is that when the parents do release them, some of these children will not have strong legs to stand on. They will fall and probably end up back with their parents because the parents did not release them step-by-step along the way.

> Adulthood is full of decisions, sacrifices, and consequences. Our job is to help the kids learn to deal with these issues before they leave home.

Letting teens drive is a major area of release. Your teen's safety is the chief concern. Please do not allow your teen to drive just because he passed his driving test or because it will make your life easier. Take the time to drive with him in a variety of circumstances to determine whether he'll be able to handle himself in any situation.

Next comes the hard part. When he is reasonably competent, give him the keys, let him go . . . and then pray! Letting our teens drive is not easy. Every time our girls drive away, I pray for their safety. And every time they go and return, they have more experience. When I was a teen, I worked in the downtown part of the city. I drove every day—in busy traffic, through all kinds of weather and construction-induced delays. Even before I was eighteen, I had gained a lot of driving experience because my parents did a good job teaching me to drive and then let me go.

Releasing is probably the most difficult part of parenting, but it will be easier when you have the right attitude.

They did the same with my sisters, yet my sisters were involved in a serious accident. They both had multiple, serious injuries that required months of recuperation. (My sisters both fully recovered.) My mom was in an extremely difficult position while she was at the hospital every day with my sisters. She had to leave me in charge of the younger two—to drive them everywhere they needed to go. I was only nineteen.

Releasing our children is not easy, but it is what God calls us to do. We do our best; then we must trust God with the outcome.

Your Attitude Is Key

I won't deny that releasing is probably the most difficult part of parenting, but it will be easier when you have the right attitude. We feel out of control (remember, control is only an illusion anyway). We have to trust God with our children. And when they are away from home, we miss them. I love being in the company of my girls. They are fun (most of the time), smart (sometimes *too* smart), exciting (unless they're in a mood), and never boring. When they are gone, I miss them. But I know they need the adventure they are experiencing. They come home with greater depth, insight into life, recharged vitality, and—my favorite—a renewed appreciation of home. I know that keeping them under my wings will cripple them.

In my heart I must acknowledge that they will never again . . . be cuddly babies, be chubby toddlers in my arms listening to stories, have the innocence of childhood that sees a potential pet in every bug, need to tell me everything that happened to them that day—because they have learned to process most of it on their own. They will no longer need me to make their snacks, tie their shoes, or drive them to all their activities.

I have done my job as the Queen Mom.

The Final Release

"This is not the end of your story," a friend reminded me as I lamented that Princess One's life wasn't unfolding in the order *I'd* planned—college, career, marriage. (Instead, she chose *her* plan of getting her own apartment, working full-time, and doing college part-time.)

God used my friend's words to show me that it's OK that my princess is living her plan even though she is not fully prepared for life on her own. Who *is*? She is growing and learning; and we have the best relationship we have had in a long time. God has a plan for her, and he is working that plan. I must remember Isaiah 55:8, 9: "'My thoughts are not your thoughts, neither are your ways my ways,' declares the LORD. 'As the heavens are higher than the earth, so are my ways higher than your ways and my thoughts than your thoughts.'"

The Lord is with Princess One constantly. Now he is the teacher, parent, and protector. I accepted that—and the peace that comes from trusting him.

• •

Well, my story isn't over, but how did the king and queen's fairy tale, *The Kingdom,* end?

The day had been brilliant. The princess's coronation over her own kingdom was beautiful. Back at the palace, the king and queen leaned back in their thrones and sighed. The king squeezed the queen's hand and winked at her.

"You've done a great job, Queen Mom. The prince and princess are strong, responsible, and confident adults. They're not perfect, but they have what they need to learn, grow, and rule their kingdoms. Yet, I can't believe the prince chose a kingdom halfway around the world."

"And what was the princess thinking when she made our court jester her Minister of Foreign Affairs?"

"Well, dear, now they are ruling their kingdoms, and we will be wise to keep our mouths shut. When they eventually realize they don't know quite everything, we'll be here to give a little advice."

"You're right. And we will pray for them to depend on the Lord—as we have—to help them rule their kingdoms and raise their families."

And they all lived happily ever after.

Royal Decree

We are not in this alone. God will honor us for our efforts. The Lord said, "Those who honor me I will honor" (1 Samuel 2:30). We are on a wild parenting ride. I don't know of anything so uncertain, consuming, difficult, and exhausting. I also don't know of anything so rewarding, satisfying, and exciting. Enjoy it!

Royal Inquiry

1. What's your initial reaction to the whole topic of releasing? How does it scare you? How does it excite you?

2. Have you ever thought much about preparing and releasing your children? Can you think of one mom who has done this well? What have you noticed that she has done that you want to emulate?

3. Honestly admit if you have trouble understanding or accepting one of your children. Why do you think this is? Did one of your parents have trouble understanding you? Use this experience to motivate you to know and accept your child.

4. Take a minute to write down what you have learned and observed about each of your children's personalities. What about their interests? Do your children need some unstructured time to think and to discover their interests?

5. How will you help your children deal with conflict in a way that prepares them for real life?

6. Will you make this commitment now? "I will from this day forward work on preparing my children for the life God planned for them, and I will take appropriate opportunities to release them in my heart and to the Lord. I am the Queen Mom. I have reclaimed my throne."

Signed—_____

Notes

Chapter 1

1. Matthew Henry, *Matthew Henry's Commentary on the Whole Bible*, 13th ed. (Peabody, MA: Hendrickson Publishers, Inc., 1991), 956.

2. Jim Weidmann and Joe White, general editors, *Parents' Guide to the Spiritual Mentoring of Teens* (Wheaton, IL: Tyndale House, 2001), 30–32.

3. Oswald Chambers, *My Utmost for His Highest* (Uhrichsville, OH: Barbour and Company, Inc., 1935, 1963), 137.

Chapter 2

1. Phil McGraw, "Tip of the Day," August 16, 2004, www.drphil.com.

2. Focus on the Family, www.family.org/welcome/aboutfof/a0000078.cfm (accessed September 16, 2004).

3. Lyric W. Winik, "Why Schools are Failing," *Parade* magazine (August 1, 2004): 16.

4. Dennis Rainey and Barbara Rainey with Bruce Nygren, *Parenting Today's Adolescent: Helping Your Child Avoid the Traps of the Preteen and Early Teen Years* (Nashville: Thomas Nelson, Inc., 1998), 255.

5. CASA, The National Center on Addiction and Substance Abuse at Columbia University, www.casafamilyday.org (accessed September 9, 2004).

Chapter 3

1. Focus on the Family Q & A, www.family.custhelp.com (accessed January 5, 2006).

Chapter 4

1. Gary Smalley, "Anger Springs from Three Separate Emotions," November 14, 2005, www.dnaofrelationships.com (accessed January 9, 2006).

Chapter 5

1. Gary Smalley, "Core Fear," May 9, 2005, www.dnaofrelationships.com (accessed January 9, 2006).

2. www.dictionary.reference.com.

3. Dennis Rainey and Barbara Rainey with Bruce Nygren, *Parenting Today's Adolescent: Helping Your Child Avoid the Traps of the Preteen and Early Teen Years* (Nashville: Thomas Nelson, Inc., 1998), 166–167.

4. Jim Weidmann and Joe White, general editors, *Parents' Guide to the Spiritual Mentoring of Teens* (Wheaton, IL: Tyndale House, 2001), 58.

Chapter 6

1. "'Helicopter' Parents," www.abcnewsstore.com, October 21, 2005 (accessed January 30, 2006).

2. Henry Cloud and John Townsend, *Boundaries* (Grand Rapids, MI: Zondervan, 1992), 75.

3. Ibid.

4. Ibid., 76.

Chapter 7

1. www.dictionary.reference.com.

2. I also recommend another book for getting the house under control—*The Messies' Manual: A Complete Guide to Bringing Order and Beauty to Your Home* by Sandra Felton (Grand Rapids, MI: Baker Publishing Group, 2005)

3. James Strong, *Strong's Exhaustive Concordance of the Bible* (Iowa Falls, IA: AMG Publishers edition by permission of World Bible Publishers, Inc., 1986), 114.

Chapter 8

1. To help you discover the person God created you to be and his plan for you, I recommend *Maximizing Your Effectiveness: How to Discover and Develop Your Divine Design* by Aubrey Malphurs (Grand Rapids, MI: Baker Books, 2006).

2. Used with permission.

Chapter 9

1. Jim Weidmann and Joe White, general editors, *Parents' Guide to the Spiritual Mentoring of Teens* (Wheaton, IL: Tyndale House, 2001), 8.

2. Larry Burkett, *Women Leaving the Workplace* (Chicago, IL: Moody Press, 1995), 14.

3. Tim Kimmel, "Loving Your Rebel," *Focus on the Family* magazine (October–November 2004): 18–19.

4. Jim Weidmann and Joe White, general editors, *Parents' Guide to the Spiritual Mentoring of Teens* (Wheaton, IL: Tyndale House, 2001), 215.

5. Ibid., 213.

6. Dennis Rainey and Barbara Rainey with Bruce Nygren, *Parenting Today's Adolescent: Helping Your Child Avoid the Traps of the Preteen and Early Teen Years* (Nashville: Thomas Nelson, Inc., 1998), 111–112.

Chapter 10

1. Ralph Woerner, "Rising Above Rebellion," *Answer* magazine (July–August 2004): 3–4.

2. My favorites are: *Personality Plus for Parents: Understanding What Makes Your Child Tick* and *Personality Plus: How to Understand Others by Understanding Yourself* by Florence Littauer, *Spirit-Controlled Temperament* by Tim LaHaye, and *The Treasure Tree* by John and Cindy Trent and Gary and Norma Smalley.

3. Florence Littauer, *Silver Boxes* (Nashville: Thomas Nelson, Inc., 1989), 146–147.

4. "Toddlerhood—Dr. Dobson Answers Your Questions: Separation Anxiety," www.focusonyourchild.com/develop/art1/A0000448.html (accessed February 22, 2006).

Meet
Brenda Garrison!

Link to her favorite resources.

Schedule a speaking engagement.

www.brendagarrison.com

FOREWORD BY SHAUNTI FELDHAHN

RLS JUST WANNA HAVE FUN TELL HER ABOUT IT CHA
F LOVE I ONLY HA███████████GU WHERE IS THE LO
EDICATED TO T█████████████E BELIEVE IN ME
AND BY YOUR█████████████IN YOUR EYES
M TOO SEXY █████████████ONDERFUL TON
OTIONAL RO█████████████H YOUR BEST
OT LOVE IS█████████████CK ME CUTS LI
KNIFE YOU'V█████████████GIVE A LITTLE BI
NK AND A SMILE ███████████DER LIVIN' ON A PR
MAN AND A WOMAN EVERYTHING I DO GROW OLD WIT

THAT CRAZY
LITTLE THING CALLED
LOVE

HE SOUNDTRACK OF MARRIAGE, SEX, AND FAITH

JUD WILHITE

STEREO

ove has a way of making people sing. Songs like "I Only Have Eyes for You," "Stand by Your Man," "Love Me Tender," and "Livin' on a Prayer" come to mind. Yet three thousand years ago, a king of Israel wrote a love song—the Song of Solomon—filled with passionate insightful principles for relationships that were true then . . . and now.

That Crazy Little Thing Called Love
ISBN 10: 0-7847-1944-6   ISBN 13: 978-0-7847-1944-2

Visit your local Christian bookstore or www.standardpub.com or call 1-800-543-1353.

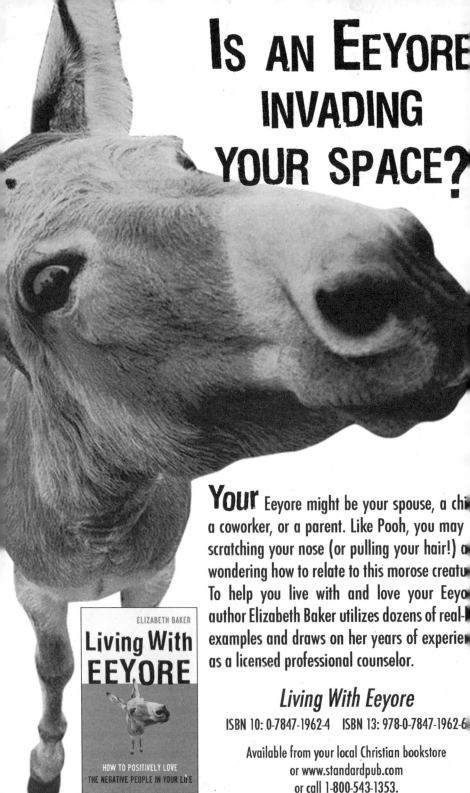